How to Win
at the
Job Game

HOW TO WIN at the JOB GAME

A Guide for Executives

Edward J Parsons

Kogan Page

Copyright © Edward J Parsons 1985

First published in Great Britain in 1985
by Kogan Page Ltd, 120 Pentonville Road, London N1 9JN
Reprinted 1985, 1986

British Library Cataloguing in Publication Data

Parsons, Edward J.
  How to win at the job game: a guide for
  executives.
  1. Job hunting   2. Executives
  I. Title
  650.1'4   HF5382.7

  ISBN 1 85091 015 4 Pb

Printed and bound in Great Britain by
Billing & Sons Limited, Worcester.

Contents

Introduction

Have you ever come into contact with, or perhaps lived next door to, a successful man? Did he have a beautiful home, two or three cars and a pony for his privately educated daughter? Did he take two foreign holidays a year, and talk of Portugal and the South of France with total acquaintance? Was his wife in a different dress every time you saw her, or didn't you notice? I'll bet your wife did!

Of course, you didn't like to pry, but where did it all come from? Family money? A good marriage? His own business?

The chances are it was none of these. Much more likely, he held down an important post as a salaried executive with a remuneration package that included a performance-related bonus, company car, personal expense account, all-inclusive family health plan, valuable life insurance, an extremely generous pension scheme, the option to buy shares in his company, and five weeks' holiday every year.

Go on. Don't be ashamed to admit it – what secretly annoyed you was that he was about the same age as you, or a bit younger, not excessively dynamic, he didn't possess an obvious 'gift of the gab' in the pub on Sunday mornings. In fact, he was so much like you that it was infuriating.

Where, then, did you differ? If you feel you would like to make an excuse at this point I can recommend one of these:

'He was lucky.' (Disbelief)
'His uncle knew the boss.' (Resignation)
'If I'd only had his opportunities.' (Fatalism)
'It's all show. That sort of chap lives on credit cards; I like to pay my way.' (Envy)
'The tobacco crop was poor in Cuba this year.' (Inventiveness)

After all, if you are going to make an excuse, any excuse will do, but you are only fooling yourself.

The one vital difference was *knowledge*.

That doesn't necessarily mean qualifications in his chosen profession. Two-thirds of the unemployed in the UK are qualified in their chosen profession. This is knowledge of a quite different kind. It comprises the very building blocks that maintain the wall between the ones that have and the ones that do not. For all its substance and the effect it has on all our lives, it is still an intangible thing without which no real progress can ever be made. The plain fact is, our successful neighbour knew how to market himself. He knew how to spot a niche in the market-place, how to develop a product to fill that niche, and how to bring that product to the buyer at a price the buyer couldn't refuse.

I know what you are asking: 'Am I too late? Can I acquire this knowledge?'

As in most things in life, if one searches long enough and is persistent, a short cut to a goal will become apparent.

This book is your short cut. Its purpose is to teach you, step by step, how to emulate the successful people you know or come in contact with. How to choose the right job in the first place. How to prepare for, and capture, that elusive position that will give you a giant push up the corporate ladder. This book will give you all the weapons you will need to fight your own personal career war. It will show you how to choose your battleground, how to assess the enemy, when to fire your broadside, and how to deliver the *coup de grâce*.

From you, the course demands two things. First, ambition. Without this, I am afraid that nothing can be done. You must truly want to better yourself and your station in life. Without this basic need, you will lack the enthusiasm to press on and overcome the obstacles. The end result will be failure. Failing is like bouncing a rubber ball that comes back, but a little less high each time, until eventually it rolls away under the garden shed and is forgotten. You need enthusiasm to pat that ball ever higher, never mind the pain in your hand and the aching shoulders, until it bounces over the wall and soars out of sight. Let us make up our minds right here. If we are going to begin, we shall carry on until the war is won. Agreed? Then let us proceed.

The second thing demanded of you is the mental capacity to accept new ideas without question. You are going to study a new approach to the jobs market. A new approach to putting yourself forward, a new approach to life. You are going to dare all, and you are going to succeed. Always remember, the tortoise only makes progress when it sticks its head out. You, however, must *want* success. You must be prepared to work until success comes. You must spend long hours in practice and preparation. How many hours, days, weeks, months, even years are spent in preparation by an Olympic athlete for that one moment, that one event that may only last a few split seconds from high board to water, or springboard to vault, yet reward the competitor with the supreme accolade?

It is not unusual for 200 people to apply for a single position. Only one can win. In 99.9 per cent of the cases, the winner is the one who prepares most thoroughly for the contest.

The first step is to start believing that the position is already yours, and to begin acting as if it were. Don't forget, you are accepting new ideas without question. Do it. Go out and buy something to wear on your first day in the new post. A new pair of shoes. Take them out each night, before bed, and brush or polish them. See yourself wearing them as you take up residence behind your new desk. I know it seems silly to you now, but it is so important to your success that this first step must not be neglected.

The second step is to start thinking analytically, assessing what you want and where you want to be, what assets you have and whether they can be used to further your career. Keep this point in mind. We are not just going to change your job for a few extra pounds a month, or get a car where none now exists. We are going to turn you into a successful, respected executive whose value will never again be in question.

In short then, the purpose of this book is to teach you how to get a better job. We will be putting great emphasis on interview techniques, what to expect, and where it will come from; how many interviews there will be and how to handle each one differently, according to its slant and the position of the interviewer. We shall deal with CVs in a radical and extended fashion, and show you how to acquire a forceful presentation that gets results. You will be shown new concepts in self-awareness and preparation that have rarely been used in this field, with the result that, on interview, you will stand out from all the rest. *You* will secretly conduct the interview, be in charge and determine the outcome. After all, why go for a job that may take you into the twenty-first century using techniques designed 50 years ago? Would you buy a ticket for the first holiday flight to the moon if you knew the journey was to be undertaken in a Tiger Moth?

Your journey is about to begin.
You have the key in your hands right now.
Put it in the ignition . . . and SWITCH ON!

Chapter 1
Analyse Yourself!

It is axiomatic that success will only come to a proponent in any field of endeavour if he or she is truly suited to that activity. It is important to study this theory from four viewpoints:

- What sort of job do you want to do?
- What can you do?
- What are you qualified to do?
- What experience have you?

What sort of job do you want to do?

At first sight, perhaps, this may be thought an obvious question, but there are still a great number of people who, every day, sift through the advertisements in an aimless fashion, following no clear-cut plan of action, replying to whichever appeals most. Quite often, the impetus to reply comes more from a subliminal appeal created by good advertising copy than a desire to enter a particular field related to present career history.

Such an application usually falls at the first hurdle, after achieving nothing except waste of the interviewer's time, fraying his temper into the bargain. It is the lack of true interest and enthusiasm that shows through, the one thing that can never be disguised or faked. You will avoid this pitfall if you ask yourself some searching questions. It is vital that you answer as truthfully as possible for your new career path to lead you in the right direction.

All you need to do is to tick the boxes if the answer is 'yes'.

Do you want to work in an office location? ☐
Would you prefer to work in the same office every day? ☐
Would you prefer to work in someone else's office? ☐
Do you like to work under constant supervision and
    guidance? ☐
Do you like to work with minimal supervision and guidance? ☑
Do you enjoy responsibility? ☑
Have you ever had to make a monthly report? ☐

Do you crave responsibility? ☑

Do you believe, with responsibility thrust upon you, that you could rise to the occasion? ☑

Do you want to be involved with production? ☐

Do you want to be involved with administration? ☐

Do you want to be involved with accounts? ☐

Do you want to be involved with sales or marketing? ☑

Do you want to work abroad? ☐

Would your spouse agree to your career decisions without question? ☑

Does your spouse have a career of his/her own? ☑

Do you believe he or she should be consulted? ☑

Would you rather work with animals than people? ☐

Do you ever read with avidity the biographies of successful people? ☐

Do you like meeting new people every day? ☑

Do you prefer to work through a clearly defined period every day? ☐

Do you find 'clocking on' degrading? ☐

Do you prefer flexible hours? ☑

Do you dislike working on Saturdays? ☐

Do you have the courage to talk to 10 strangers every day? ☑

Do you strike up friendships easily? ☑

Could you be unkind to your best friend if it were necessary? ☑

Do you enjoy making things with your hands? ☐

Do you enjoy working at painstaking tasks week after week? ☐

Would you prefer to change assignments every day? ☐

Would you prefer to change assignments every hour? ☐

Do you like to work under great pressure? ☐

Do you prefer a quiet business life? ☐

Would you prefer to be paid a straight salary? ☐

Would you prefer to be paid on a commission-only basis, but earn more money than a straight salary? ☐

Would you prefer a mix of salary and commission? ☑

Have you ever sold anything to a stranger? ☐

Did you enjoy it? ☐

Did you make a profit? ☐

Do you enjoy working with figures and specifications? ☑

Are you creative? ☐

Are you artistic? ☑

Are you technically minded? ☐

Are you an original thinker? ☑

Are you a doer, rather than a talker? ☑

There are, of course, no right or wrong answers. What we are looking for are trends. You may find that you crave responsibility, prefer flexible hours, like working Saturdays, want to work in other people's offices, under pressure on commission only. The most obvious career suggested by this profile would be in the insurance industry. A preference for figures and specifications, irregular hours, responsibility, straight salary, minimal supervision and guidance in an office location could suggest a career as a quantity surveyor or purchasing officer.

The permutations are endless, but you have achieved an important step. By putting pen to paper, you have concentrated your mind, brought your desires into the open and examined them in a good light. Having now decided on the kind of job you want, the next step is to discover whether or not you are capable of doing it.

What can you do?

Another obvious question, but there is no point in aiming for the top, actually getting the job, only to be fired three months later because you are totally out of your depth. It is not necessary that one should have held down a similar post in the past and been effective in it. To make sure, as far as anyone can, that one can do the job, one only needs to have operated on the fringes of that job, with perhaps delegated or occasional responsibility in a similar discipline: to have put oneself on a probationary test period, as it were, and to have the inner confidence that comes from knowing that one could have performed a more responsible task quite efficiently and without stress. At this juncture, then, we shall compile another list, looking back over your career and writing down every occasion you can recall where you assumed authority or it was delegated to you. You will list every opportunity where you were able to demonstrate executive or management skills and in what area that opportunity occurred.

At the end of the list, you should have a fairly accurate idea of the various disciplines in which you have had experience of responsibility, no matter if it was only for an hour, where you can truly say, 'I was in control of that' or, 'My actions in that situation resulted in an improvement.'

What are you qualified to do?

It is difficult to assess the importance of qualifications to your prospective employer. Obviously, if you wish to design circuit boards, or work with stress factors on steel, or possibly study the flow of fluids over solid objects, then a certain level of qualification is required and there will be set levels that are recognized in your industry. There are, however, many areas where qualifications are nebulous. Let's look at what they are trying to prove.

The employer is looking for the person of the highest calibre that he can buy for the amount of money he is prepared to spend. Therefore, when he advertises for new staff, he will ask for degrees, HNC, ONC, A levels, trade qualifications: everything that can hypothetically be crammed into one person. He does not expect that one body will appear on his office threshold equipped with all those qualifications plus all the other qualities he seeks, with the burning yen to work for him, and him alone. At best he will hope that one or two people will emerge from what will possibly be a fairly unexciting selection at least to present him with a choice. I believe it has never occurred that a man who was suitable for a post in every other respect has not been offered it when his only shortcoming has been lack of qualifications, where those asked for were of a non-technical nature.

A word of warning must be given here. Never put in an application form, or claim at interview, qualifications that you do not possess. The chances are you will be asked for proof on the day that you join the company if not before, and without them your departure will be faster than your arrival. Furthermore, you will have damaged beyond repair both your professional reputation and your confidence. If you feel that the possession of qualifications is of such overwhelming importance, and you have none, it is better to choose a different job than to lead your prospective employer wildly astray with untruths in your application form. To infer certain levels of knowledge, where the inference is drawn further by the interviewer is, of course, a different matter entirely. We shall be dealing with this at a later stage.

What experience have you?

This subject is very similar to qualifications. Again, an employer would much prefer to be able to take on somebody who is so experienced in the line of work that the applicant would be able to step straight into the shoes of his predecessor, and be so well versed in that discipline as to effect the switch in personnel without those around him being aware of the change. This hardly ever happens. Human nature being what it is, there are always changes, no matter how experienced the new man is. In many cases, the person appointed may be the right man, although lacking previous experience, but because of his other qualities it would be felt that he could handle the job. When he actually takes possession of the desk, in the early days he is very much reliant upon those around him to make sure that the transition is smooth.

When presented with a CV listing many years' experience in a particular position, an interviewer acquaintance of mine would always ask, 'Is this 20 years' experience, Mr Jones, or one year of experience repeated 20 times over?'

This is a very valid point. For someone to say he was in a job for 10 years and can therefore bring 10 years' experience to the new post is not always a recommendation. Most senior executives tend to look upon their jobs as short-term tasks. When they begin in a position, they will happily state that it is a fantastic job, with all the challenge and demands upon them that they could wish for. If they are still behind the same desk three years later, however, then it will be a boring, lack-lustre task indeed, heavy with the aura of being passed over for the next move up the corporate ladder. They will have acquired only two to three years' experience in that particular job, but the point is well made. After that, they are ready for new fields to plough: new responsibilities, higher authority. That amount of experience is more than enough for the upwardly mobile executive to succeed in a position, and make his mark on those above him.

The third important point regarding experience is how you can link yours to the type of job you are seeking. This is where you are looking back over your career, searching for a connection, no matter how tenuous, between what you have done and what you want to do. For instance, you may once have worked for a company that had as its main customer one of the largest manufacturers in the UK, a company whose name would carry great weight with your prospective employer. At interview and in your CV you will make greater mileage out of your association with the main customer than with your employer at that time, thereby creating and establishing a link between your past experience and what your new employer would want you to do.

It is true that people love to deal with successful people. If your interviewer feels that you have worked with a company in some area, even if it is only a loose connection, comparable or better than his own, then the experience question will be bypassed and you will be on to the next step. Search, then, for the links in your career, the companies you have been associated with, that you can mention at first instance when you are discussing your new post. Such experience is invaluable.

How to write a job specification for yourself

Pick up a newspaper, any newspaper. You will probably find an advertisement in the sits vacant section that is headed along the lines of:

DO YOU FIT THIS PROFILE?

or:

CAN YOU MATCH THIS BLUEPRINT OF A
SUCCESSFUL EXECUTIVE?

It will then continue:

> 'The man we are seeking will be aged 35-45, energetic, enthusiastic, well qualified, capable of doing this, that or the other, with x number of years' experience in this or that discipline . . . ' and so on, until you get to the end of the advertisement where it will state: 'If you think you match up, ring Terry on . . . '.

What we have just read is, to all intents and purposes, a job specification. First of all, someone in Personnel or an outside consultancy, the MD, or even a departmental manager, has sat down to write exactly what the successful applicant will have to do. This is a job specification. It will be the Bible by which the new man or woman will be measured. From that job spec he is able to write a description of the sort of person able to do the new job. For example, if the job description requires 10 calls to be made in a day, then he will be looking for evidence of industriousness from his candidates. If you had shown a history of sales where four or five calls a day were the norm, then you would have placed a barrier between yourself and the position that might prove impossible to remove. On the other hand, taking along to the interview your call record sheets showing a consistent call rate of a dozen calls a day would be more than sufficient proof that your assiduity matched the profile written, placing you in a very strong position indeed.

Using that as an example, write a job specification for yourself that will fit your qualifications and personal profile exactly. Start with your age, previous experience, qualifications, all the items that you will see mentioned in a rudimentary search of half a dozen 'senior executive wanted' advertisements.

Do not rely on the first specification that you write. Study it. Refine it. Enlarge its areas. Paint with a broad brush. Remember, the wider the appeal, the wider the personal profile, then the more jobs may be considered in your search for employment or promotion. Once the specification is written, it is a simple task to start comparing your specification with advertisements to see where your qualifications match those asked for by a prospective employer. Furthermore, it is not unheard of for you to send your personal profile to a personnel consultancy for their opinion as to which area of industry they think you would be most suited. You can also ask your business contacts and office colleagues for advice. Tackle it on these lines: your neighbour, who is employed at present (it is most important that you make that point), is looking for advancement, but is undecided whether to continue on his present career path (note the choice of words – we shall come back to this point at a later stage), diversify, or concentrate his experience into one particular area. Then ask your colleague, or whoever you are addressing, to suggest one or two positions for which he might feel this mythical person to be suited.

Never forget, people love to be asked for their advice. It makes them feel good, warm, human and important, and they will very rarely ever refuse. This is a very important personality trait in humans that you must learn to make use of. It is well known that Henry Ford was asked by a Congressional committee to show why he should be considered fit to run such an influential corporation, given his rudimentary education. He simply replied that on his desk were six buttons. He had only to press one to bring an expert to the office, versed in any corporate subject they could name. He could then ask that expert's advice, and make an informed decision. With this ploy, and a very honest ploy it was, he was able to convince the committee that no better hands could hold the destiny of America's motor industry so securely.

He knew how to get information, he knew how to ask for advice, and he used this knowledge indefatigably.

Do you want to do it?

You should now have in front of you a list of jobs gained from your researches, fitting your job specification and personality profile as accurately as you can make it. This is most important. If you are not satisfied, or doubt in any way the accuracy of your information, then do it again. Repeat the exercise. When you eventually face the interviewer, it will be because he has already matched the personality profile in your CV against his job specification. If you have aimed for the wrong job because your spec and profile were wrong, then you will not get to interview, or if you do, then you will not be successful. Much valuable time will be lost, and a sorry experience undergone that could have been avoided.

Likewise, when you study the list of jobs for which you are suited, you must decide which of them you do not want to do. You may be suited for a job in the construction industry, possibly in site management, but if you don't like walking over building sites in the depths of a freezing winter, or trying to converse with a gang of labourers whose only desire is to finish the job as quickly as possible and make a beeline for the nearest warm public bar, then you would be advised to go for your second or third choice.

Unless you are totally enthusiastic and prepared to be devoted to your new occupation, you will not make a success of it. This cannot be stressed too highly. Everyone goes through a honeymoon period when they begin a new job. Every day is exciting. One is meeting new people with personalities so different from what one is used to. The possibilities of advancement appear endless. Three months later, when the newness has worn off and things are not going as they should be, you have become just another employee whose dreams are never to be fulfilled because the love of the task is just not there, the realisation has arrived that a serious error of judgement has been made, and a step taken away from a planned and successful progression along your career path.

Make sure, then, before you start to apply for your new job, that your enthusiasm and desire to work in that area are such that you just cannot envisage life without it. You must eat, sleep and drink that new position. You must go about your business as if you have already secured it, and made a marriage that will endure above all.

Balancing character against the stars

No one has ever explained satisfactorily the link between a person's character and the star sign under which he was born. That link, however, in a high percentage of cases, appears with such consistency that its existence cannot be denied. Even the sceptics among you must put away your doubts for the moment and accept another new and radical idea without question. You must seek an informed volume (your local library will help with this) and study the characteristics of your star sign. There will be both good and bad points to contend with. Do not close your eyes to the negative features of your personality. Acknowledge their presence, recognize them in yourself and make a genuine effort to eradicate them or, if this is not possible in the time allowed, be constantly alert throughout the selection period that these traits do not manifest themselves. For example, some Sagittarians show a low level of social tolerance. They might not like to admit it, but the trait is there. You would be ill-advised to give even a hint of your prejudice to your interviewer: the risks run from being asked to do business in the future with ethnic groups, to his wife being of a different race or creed.

Study your character, be forewarned, and choose your job wisely with the information you have extracted about yourself very much in mind.

Analyse your handwriting

Many companies in the last decade relied on the expert opinion of a graphologist to study a sample of the applicant's handwriting and give an informed assessment of his capacity to perform in the post applied for. A lot of weight was attached to the graphologist's opinion, and many careers came to a halt because of it. While not so popular as it was, there is no doubt that the practice still exists, so it is as well to devote a few evenings to the problem, again with the help of the local library. Of all the subconscious ways we reveal our personality, none is more accurate than our handwriting, although others, such as body language, are equally effective. Handwriting has the advantage of being available to the analyst for a period of time, to allow careful and complete study.

Once written and presented, the sample cannot be changed. This die is cast. Application of simple principles, however, will weight the scales more in your favour. Do you want to present the appearance of being a go-getter, decisive and positive, in command of the situation and a definite leader of men? To include every characteristic of this personality in your handwriting would be foolish, and so remarkable as to appear unreal. To make sure that you always cross your t with a straight stroke, dot the i two or three letters forward, and lean your uprights forward with no twiddly bits on the down stroke is not, however, too much to ask or remember. Use a broad-nib pen and not a ball-point, roller-ball or felt-tip, and the difference will be both remarkable and successful.

The second most important point about assuming the writing characteristics of a stronger personality (or a more gentle one if that is your desire) is that in a very short time one will assume these characteristics and undergo a personality change. This is because, as we write and strive to remember these points and reproduce them on the page, the desire to change is sinking into our subconscious and taking root, changing us all the time, gently but surely. This is a powerful weapon at our disposal when trying to influence a person – perhaps never seen – who will assess the letter of application or handwriting sample. Don't forget, even people with no experience whatever in graphology, with no wish to submit your text to analysis, will not fail to be favourably impressed by a firm progressive writing style. It is another basic human trait that you are now aware of. Use it.

Discover as much about yourself as you can

The reason for this personality programme is simple. Your interviewer is going to try and discover as much as is humanly possible about you with a view to paying you a large sum of money to do a job for him. He will use any technique – real, tested or imagined – to prove to himself that he is not making a mistake, until he is convinced that you fit all the different shapes as tightly as possible. When that moment of conviction arrives, he will offer you the job, and it will take heaven and earth to make him change his mind.

Your aim is to hide your bad qualities as far out of his sight as possible, while putting your best assets in front of him so forcefully that he will make the buying decision sooner rather than later. Unless you know yourself inside out, the wrong points will be emphasized, his vision diverted, and the opportunity lost. No chance must be left for him to know more about you than you do.

Are women at a disadvantage in the job market?

Since the advent of women's liberation, it has often been brought to public attention that a woman needs to be many times better than a man just to get a fair chance at doing a comparable job. I do not believe this to be so. In a worth-while company, every job is available to those who can convince the interviewer that they are capable of doing it better than the other applicants, and fit for promotion to higher things when the task is fulfilled. It is not generally realized that the second point is of equal or even greater importance when selecting executives than the first.

It is here that the ladies have not succeeded. They fail to understand the game, not the rules. Have no fear. When you have read this book, and put into practice all that you have been taught, your chances of success in business will be vastly improved.

At the end of each chapter, a checklist will summarise the important points and give you a chance to ensure that all have been assimilated; if in doubt, read this chapter again before proceeding to the next. Without covering the suggested work schedule completely, you will be unable to progress.

Checklist

1. Do you know what you want to do?
2. Are you capable of doing it?
3. Can you meet the question of qualification head-on, and win?
4. Do you have experience of the tasks you seek?
5. Have you constructed a satisfactory personality profile?
6. Have you researched other people's opinions of your capabilities?
7. Do you have a burning desire to perform your chosen task above all others?
8. Do you know yourself better than ever before?
9. Do you like what you know?
10. Can you honestly reply 'yes' to every question?

Then turn the page. You are ready for the next step.

Nine yes's or less? Shame on you. Start again, but work late. We don't have much time to spare.

Chapter 2
Looking for an Opening

We are now equipped to start the search for the right position. Our profile and job specification are complete, we know more about ourselves than ever before, and the way ahead is clear for some positive decisions. What is the next step?

Where to look for the job you want

Paradoxically, where to look for a job is not a problem. Jobs are all around you. Every company in the country is looking for a person who can fill a position of worth, and whose input will fully justify the company's expenditure on them by advancing the position of that company in the market-place.

The most obvious places are the national and local press, trade magazines, personnel consultancy lists, advertisements on local radio, in-house journals and magazines of large companies, professional association newsletters, university careers offices and governmental Jobcentre publications such as *PER (Professional and Executive Recruitment)*.

A secondary line of contact with employment is to make use of people you know who would be prepared to give you an introduction to their personnel department or, if they are in suitably advanced positions themselves, able to offer a post in their company, always bearing in mind the golden rule, 'Never work for friends or relations'.

It may seem like a good idea at the time to ask your brother-in-law or uncle, for example, for a job but, human nature being what it is, when an argument ensues – and make no mistake, it always will occur – your boss will suddenly find himself in the invidious position of having to reprimand a relative or friend, making a decision doubly difficult. The result is often over-reaction, with your new job suffering in the process.

The third most important area involves creating a position that you would like to occupy.

Job creation

There are a number of people who go through life with a burning desire or ambition. It may take the form of scaling new heights, plumbing new ocean depths, subjecting themselves to ever more tortuous physical strain or stress but, for a small sector, that desire takes the form of working with a particular person or company, or on a specific project. For our mythical man or woman, no suitable position may be advertised at the time of looking. He or she will have to create their own job. This is not as difficult as it may seem. One simply needs to isolate, very accurately, the position that one seeks, and follow it up by the construction of a job specification. After putting the most common title to the specification, for example 'Research and Development Director' or 'Product Planning Manager', an approach to the company in question, bearing in mind that one needs to penetrate no further than the switchboard or reception, will ascertain if the position exists and whether it is occupied. If the position is not filled, or no job currently exists, the way forward is open for one to contact the director under whose authority one would be engaged, and present the case for taking the idea on board. Once the possibilities and cost effectiveness of future action are demonstrated, there is every chance of the candidate being engaged.

Unsuccessful at the first attempt? Ask why. You will be told. The next question is: 'If I can overcome that objection to your complete satisfaction, is there any reason why your company should not engage me there and then?'

If the answer is 'No', overcome the objection and you have achieved the impossible. If the answer is 'Yes', discover the next objection, overcome that, and proceed to the closing step.

All too easy, did you say? Of course it is. That is why you bought the book. You wanted a quick way to success. Be brave, persistent and keep an open mind, and nothing will restrict your progress.

That is job creation in its purest form, and it is often a worth-while method, shunned by the faint-hearted, of finding employment in the more esoteric areas open to executives with a technical or scientific bent.

The secret of success in this method is to make sure that you are approaching the man who will make the decision. Any further down the pecking order, and you will scare the daylights out of some somnambulistic paper shuffler who is cruising to retirement with as little intention of making waves as possible. If you cannot get to this manager on his own ground, then plot and scheme to meet him socially. Your aim is to present your case, make an ally of him, and give him something to 'take upstairs' that will not only be of real worth to the company, but enhance his reputation as a manager of superior business acumen. With such a man on your side, you have crossed the main hurdle of job creation. After that, adhering to the simple methods explained in this book will ensure that the position is yours.

A word of warning, however, on where to direct your attack, is called for at this time.

Don't go in at the bottom

There is a tendency among the shyer element to feel that, if they can get a job, any job, in an organization, they will be able to prove their worth in a short time, and work their way up. This is possible, but very hit and miss and no sure route to executive success. While you are busy working your way out of the post room, or a boring order-taking job calling on 20 shops a day, you could have started five years further along the promotion path as an administration manager or sales and marketing manager. If you set your sights high, and use the correct techniques to obtain that job, you will, at a stroke, dispose of many dreary years spent trying to prove your worth. There is no reason at all why the series of interviews you will be asked to attend should not form the arena in which to display your talents. That is what they are for.

Never forget another golden rule in business: your standing will never be higher in a company in the early days than when you first join it. You will be able to request the impossible, and get it, if you can show you need it to perform the task for which you were employed. This is only because your new boss is impressed with *his* decision to employ you.

Give him the chance to feel that way in advance, by showing your talents at the beginning, instead of running for cover and hoping that he will discover them quite by chance. Be assured he will not. He will not have the time, being too busy looking after the person who got the job you should have had. There is no virtue in saying, 'I have worked for this company, man and boy, for 30 years,' and still being only half-way to your goal. You will have missed your chance, waiting either for dead men's shoes or for somebody at board level to notice your efforts and reward them.

Time passes too quickly. Five years can whizz by in an office environment, if you are in a rut. For an executive not to notice your efforts from one year to the next is not so unusual. You cannot blame him. You have taken on the appearance of moving wallpaper, a not very important cog in his machine. Worse still, the head of department may change, leaving you as one of yesterday's men.

Pick your spot, therefore, and aim at it carefully. Use a rifle, not a shotgun. Precision pays.

Go for a position of high vulnerability. Do not settle for a quiet spot where, if you keep your head down, and nose clean, you can live out the rest of your working days behind your desk with total security.

That, I can assure you, is all you will ever achieve. Look around you. Study what the dynamic executives in your company are doing. They are putting themselves in the front line every day. They are constantly talking about 'high profile' or 'up at the sharp end'. If their jobs are not that open to attack, they are constantly striving to give the opposite impression. Only when you are seen to be performing well in difficult circumstances or under 'great pressure' will you be noticed and rewarded with promotion or a better financial package.

Unfortunately, no matter how hard you strive or play the 'executive game', it is very difficult to boost a nonentity of a job in the eyes of your superiors. Very little excitement ever occurs at the bottom of the ladder. Ask any apprentice. All they ever get is the droppings from those above as they look up.

Go in as high up as you can possibly reach, then fight like a madman to maintain your finger-hold until you can drag yourself up to a more secure position. If necessary, jump for that first grasp. The higher you jump, the more secure will be your grip, and the better the ultimate reward.

Getting a job is like fighting a war

You are now ranged against the forces of opposition and they are mighty indeed. With massive, worldwide unemployment and companies striving to replenish their profits before spending more on the payroll, they need to be certain that the person they take on board is going to be a true asset to their company, and that he will earn his salary many times over. The cost of replacing a bad choice within three months of appointment can easily reach twice the outgoing executive's salary per annum, no mean sum.

What equipment do you need to fight and win?

To become involved in this executive battle, you need certain equipment. If you are to stand any chance of winning, your equipment must be of the highest quality. It must be constantly serviced and maintained, updated and renewed. Certain items that you need in your armoury are indispensable. Extra weaponry would probably conclude the engagement sooner, but the ultimate result is still winning. Let us list a number of weapons applicable to this battle, in no specific order of importance:

- A track record in your particular field.
- Qualifications.
- A stable career history.
- A good general education.
- Specific experience of the position sought.

- Knowledge of the disciplines involved in carrying out that work effectively.
- Formal business training.
- Possession of a well developed sense of self-reliance and persistence.
- The ability to work under pressure.
- The ability to accept the imposition of targets and consistently achieve them.
- The ability to function as a team member within a chain of command.
- The age and physical presence to command the attention and gain the respect of one's peers.
- The ability to negotiate, liaise and present to decision makers.
- Previous experience of responsibility for a subordinate's output.

Quite obviously, if you possessed all those attributes you probably would not need this book. You would be on a 'headhunter' list in your industry with your future assured, or subject to constant improvement in your package to stop you looking further than your present employer. This book is for those who lack some or most of the qualities. From the list, you cannot do without self-reliance, persistence, and the ability to work under pressure with others. Nowadays it is considered of paramount importance that the incoming employee should react favourably with the incumbent team members. His ability to function as a team member is often one of the prime causes of his promotion or acceptance. Let us limit the choice even further: a reader has checked the list with devastating honesty and realised that he possesses none of the stated qualities. Is he therefore doomed?

Of the important qualities, only one has been omitted, but that is the most important of all. Without it, all else is of little use. That quality is enthusiasm. If you could pick just one weapon only, then unflagging enthusiasm for the product, for success, for the company, for the people around you, would gain the day. Make no mistake, there is more than one senior executive who now appears fully equipped to cope with any business decision or problem that may arise, who initially began his career armed only with enthusiasm, with a burning light that shone through and let everyone around him know that with this man they just could not fail.

A good employment record showing stability and honesty is better in some cases than a track record in the particular discipline in which you intend to function. Many a man is chosen to perform a task, for example, in marketing, dealing with a product of which he has no experience whatsoever: that man has been employed for his talents as a marketing executive, not for his knowledge of the product. The company has, without doubt, many dozens of people who can be relied upon to supply technical back-up at the press of a button. So do not despair.

If you appear to be the one person who can do the job, you will achieve the position no matter what your background. I may even say that more than a few of the boardrooms in this country do not lack executives with some pretty frightening skeletons in their cupboards, including theft and dishonesty on varying scales. When they joined the company, their interviewers were so impressed that they were prepared to take those people on without checking their references too deeply. It is a source of wonderment to me that this practice still persists. Never, ever, should you employ somebody without first checking their references.

If you do not like what you hear, you can then reappraise the situation, and you may well decide to employ the person anyway, but at least you have some insight into their previous work history. However, this simple precaution by the employer seems destined never to be followed without exception, and therein lies hope. It is most important to recognize and believe that there will always be a second chance. Some of you reading this will be of the opinion that, because of a stupid mistake, you will probably never work again. Not a bit of it! Perseverance, guts, determination and enthusiasm will ensure that you will be back in the executive world very shortly, and if you treat your employer with the honesty that he has shown you, those skeletons will eventually be buried for ever.

If industry has one point to its credit, it is that it takes a man or woman into a company on face value and judges them on their merits. Very rarely will you come across companies that indulge in nepotism. 'Do the stuff, and you will be rewarded' is probably the finest maxim that you can write above your desk.

What are the arms ranged against you?

You are, or will be at the end of this book, well equipped to charge into battle but there will be obstacles that you must surmount. They will take the form of the employer's desire to find the best person for the job. They will also include your own deficiencies which will work against you as long as you possess them. Let us look at the employer first.

To understand his weapons, we need to understand why he is using them. The employer has one aim in life, and one aim only: he wants to find somebody who will complete the task as well as he would complete it himself. For this effort, because he plans to delegate the responsibility, he is prepared to pay money. The better you can convince him that you can perform this task, and others besides, then the greater your reward will be. As his company increases in size the more people he needs to employ. No one will ever be scrutinized so closely as the first employee that man takes on because he is involving himself in delegation for the first time. The larger the company grows, then the further the task of delegation is removed from the company's head, and the easier it becomes to obtain employment in that company. It is a fallacy to believe that the bigger the company, the tougher it is to join. The same principles will always apply. Prove your worth, and the job will be yours. In competition, prove you are better suited than the next man.

Ranged against you will be all the techniques that personnel departments use to filter out the unwanted and undesirable. You will encounter interviews – one to one or with a group; personality tests; you will be asked to provide references; perhaps a handwritten letter for analysis; maybe a behavioural psychologist will sit in to study your reaction to stress by body-language interpretation; you may be presented with group activity where set problems are solved by a group of candidates, the group being analysed for the production of natural leaders who perform well in a team environment. It is fairly common these days to employ personnel consultants to perform the initial weeding out, all with specially developed techniques of their own. They are expert in spotting the smallest signs that the interviewee displays indicating a possible success or failure further down the line and are able to discard him or her without damage to their vulnerable reputations. Remember, the consultant's future with the client is on the line every time he puts a name forward for consideration. He has to be exceedingly careful if he wants to stay in a cutthroat business with an ongoing client base.

Fortunately, against all the arms you have prepared a shield. This shield is your job specification and personality profile. Having worked so meticulously in preparing it, you will be able to deflect any barb shot at you in an interview. You will be prepared for the board interview, rather than the one-to-one. You will be ready to display and prove your worth, to demonstrate your plans for the job, because you have researched deeply and already know how to overcome these particular problems. An ounce of preparation in these circumstances will prove to be worth a ton of improvisation.

Subjective influences and how to overcome them

There is one influence on your prospective success, however, that you cannot control beforehand with such precision. We have been dealing with objective influences. Now we must talk about the subjective: this nebulous area where, when two strangers meet, the chemistry between them causes a balance to be struck, either favourable or otherwise. If the balance is unfavourable, the uninitiated to job-hunting success will leave the interview feeling very uneasy, and two weeks later a letter will appear on the mat with a brief message of 'Thanks, but no thanks'. There is only one way to overcome the subjective influence in an interview: get the interviewer on your side. Let us paint a broad canvas to illustrate.

On entering the room, it becomes apparent almost immediately that your interviewer is of the brusque, tight-lipped variety. From his initial gaze and frown, he has obviously found something he doesn't like, unless he is just trying to unsettle you. There is no way of knowing at this early stage. What you do know is that you prefer to deal with the happy, suave, laid-back person who goes out of his way to put you at ease. You sink in your seat with your heart somewhere in your boots. After trying for 10 minutes to crack his reserve, you can feel the whole thing just slipping away from you, disastrously.

For this, and every other type of human personality interaction problem, there is a staggeringly simple solution.

Adopt his posture. If he sits in the chair with his legs crossed and his arms folded, do likewise. If he then uncrosses his legs and puts his hands in his lap, do likewise. If he then hunches forward and clasps his hands in front of him on the desk, do likewise. Every posture that the man employs, copy exactly. Do not do it immediately. A couple of seconds after will suffice, but ensure that you are mirroring his posture. You will begin to see a change in some cases. His attitude will become more friendly. If there is no change, it does not mean that he is not more friendly disposed towards you, simply that you need to ascertain his level of friendliness. You will now instigate a change in posture. Your interviewer should follow suit and adopt your posture. If he does, you will know that you have won him over, and you have succeeded in getting him well disposed towards you. If he does not move, then assume his posture and try again a few minutes later. Persistence will bring its own reward. I guarantee, no matter who it is, this appeal to his subconscious will be successful, and you will win him over, and make a friend of him, even though he is not aware of it. That is one of the basic laws of psychology and will stand you in good stead for ever more.

Conservatism in industry rules

It is a valid point, constantly reinforced by interviewers' comments after a hard day spent seeing unsuitable people, that most of the subjective influences brought against candidates are of their own making. They often take the form of dislike for the candidate's appearance and can so easily be avoided.

The rule is, and always will be, conservatism rules! It is no good complaining that it is a free world and that people should be prepared to take you as they find you. It isn't and they needn't. You are coming to play their game on their pitch. If you refuse to wear the right strip, or ignore the basic rules, you cannot complain if you are sent off. I do not care what the current fashion is, extremes of dress and behaviour are not acceptable in a business environment, and never will be. The girl who dresses to seduce her interviewer into giving her the job will surely fail. His reaction will be one of embarrassment, not desire, and the interview will be terminated quickly. If he cannot trust the girl with him, how can he trust her with his best customer? Likewise the man who arrives in the latest jeans, sandals, and sunglasses. It just will not do, and I venture to suggest that we all know it. Attitudes in industry are set by its leaders, and they are invariably middle aged, so expect middle-aged attitudes to prevail. It has a purpose, after all. Stability is maintained at all levels, and industry can prevail in a constant atmosphere. Without this consistency, there would be no jobs to apply for. It all comes down to mental attitude, which is as good a place as any to take us into the next step.

Checklist

1. Have you started to look for a new job?
2. Will you choose job creation?
3. Remember to aim high. How high dare you go?
4. Are you starting to use the rifle instead of the shotgun approach?
5. How many weapons do you have in your armoury?
6. Are you enthusiastic?
7. Are you aware of the arms ranged against you?
8. Have you practised controlling the subjective influences?
9. Do you have a conservative attitude towards the business environment?

Chapter 3

Clean up Your Act!

If anyone had the time to conduct an exhaustive survey to discover the main reason why candidates fail interviews and selection boards, they would undoubtedly find it to be the person's mental attitude. It is something that gives us away: we cannot fake a positive mental attitude. Although we may strive to keep alert, bouncy, bright, enthusiastic and dynamic, the intense pressure of the pretence and the subtly different but equal strain of a drawn out interview situation will eliminate all but the strongest willed. Don't gamble on your will-power. Get your mental attitude right, and give yourself one problem less to deal with.

Mental attitude

There are a number of aspects to building up a strong positive mental attitude, but without belief you are conquered before the battle has begun. You must *believe* in the rightness of what you are attempting: that is why you had so much to do in the previous chapters. You have already proved to yourself that you can get where you want to be by a simple but deep examination of your own powers. Now there is no obstacle to your belief in the rightness of your chosen path.

You must believe in your own ultimate success. A wise sales manager with years of experience in training raw salesmen asked his newest recruit where he was going the next day. He replied, 'I'm going to call on Smith and Son again.' His manager then asked, 'Will you get the order?' The salesman, not wishing to push his commitment too far only to appear foolish, said, 'I'm not sure.' 'Then why waste £75 of company money? If you are not going to close the sale, why bother going back?'

The moral is obvious. You must believe in your success first. *Before* it happens. Only then will it become a reality. Why? Because your mental attitude will communicate itself to those around you. They will ultimately be carried along on your wave of enthusiasm. Their momentum will add to yours and you will be unstoppable. Your mind will be agile, sharp, with a heightened awareness that you are keeping your finger on the very pulse of the situation. Heavens above, how can you possibly fail with all this going for you! I'm getting excited just writing about it. Consider this point. How would you feel if you had just been told that you had won the football pools, or been promoted to managing director of your company? Are there strong enough words in the thesaurus to describe your joy, your transports, the cold prickle that will run up the back of your neck and raise hairs on your scalp as you lie in bed, dog-sharp, planning your future until the dawn arrives, sleep long since dismissed as an unattainable irrelevance.

Go back to the beginning of the book. Seek out the passage in the introduction that begins, 'The second thing demanded of you is the mental capacity to accept new ideas without question,' and copy it out. Write large on a sheet of A4 and place it on a wall where it can be seen the moment you wake and as you lie down to sleep, and read it. Read it every morning and night, aloud, until it is embedded in your subconscious. Put another copy under your pillow. You will feel silly? Your wife will laugh at you? Will they mock when the ultimate prize is yours? Don't question it, do it. Do it now!

Now is also the time to go out and buy that item we spoke about. I have always chosen shoes because of their help to me in concentrating. Buy the best pair of black shoes you can afford. If you are unemployed and money is short, then save. Give up something. Sacrifice. I don't care what you do, just get those shoes. Polish them every night until they glow like a burnished shield, reflecting all your wishes and desires. Talk to them as you polish, tell them that you are going to achieve your aims, and that they are going to help you. Put them under your bed at night, facing north to south, but do not put them on.

Why north to south? I do not want to confuse you with too many new ideas at once, but we are moving along the fringes of parapsychology when we use the subconscious to influence decisions. One of the tenets of this branch of science is that natural forces that endow or stimulate the subconscious, move in a north/south direction, similar to magnetic waves.

They are for the first day in your new job. If you wear them beforehand, the link will be broken and your attempt will fail. Once again, do not be embarrassed by these actions. You are simply using the power of your subconscious to influence those around you. This is not a new technique. It is not a very well understood technique, either, and sceptics will mock and scoff until the end of time, but it works. Believe me, it works!

'I can't abide that man. He's a right idiot.' How many times have you said that? Once? A hundred times? Even a thousand? Shame on you. You will never be successful. You will never get that job with a mental attitude coloured by criticism. You must learn that all successful people who want to rise to management have, eventually, to be respected by their colleagues and liked by their subordinates. You always thought you had to be ruthless to get on? You do, but not at the expense of other people's feelings. To be ruthless with life, with problems, with obstacles, that is the way forward. To be gentle with people as you pass them on your way up, that is godliness.

Determination must also figure large in your mental make-up, now. With this is concentrated will-power, the ability to see things through, to get tasks done, to preserve enthusiasm at its highest peak. Do not worry if your life has been a history of failed chances and opportunities missed. It happens to most people. The problem is the lack of a simple method to acquire all of the above traits. It does not exist. No philosopher has ever discovered the complete answer to that problem, but there is an answer that exists on a different plane. That plane is action.

If you take action, things get done. If you take swift, decisive action, things get done quickly. You do not need sustained will-power and stamina to cope with thinking about things as well as doing them. You do not need to keep your enthusiasm at its height just to help you face the worries. Somewhere, in your car (a favourite spot used by successful people is on the speedometer) put a small strip of sticky tape. On this tape write in capitals, so you can always see it clearly, 'DO IT NOW'. Let these be your watchwords, one of your mottoes for life, and success will come knocking before you are even ready for it.

Physical appearance

So you want to be an executive. Do you look like one? Do you know what one looks like? Are they the same in the office as they are on the street? Behind closed doors, do they slump around in braces with their collars undone, sleeves rolled up to the biceps, hair awry? Are their socks at half-mast and their shoes dirty and unlaced? Are their nails bitten and unkempt, their fingers golden with the nicotine of a thousand hurried cigarettes? Are their shoulders slumped beneath a crumpled suit, shiny with wear and baggy at knee and elbow? Be cruel to yourself, and ask, are you any of these things? Let us begin at the beginning, and remember, this does not apply to men only. This book has been written to help women succeed equally, so the same rules apply.

When two people meet, each is presented with a vertical line on their horizon. It is only natural that the eye should travel, in the first instance, from one extremity to another, and so it does. All the viewer will look at are your hair and your shoes. Some people refer to this as 'looking you up and down'. They are searching for a focal point that will be inoffensive, that will concentrate their gaze on you without embarrassment to either.

Let us deal with the ends of the line first. There is no alternative, your hair must be immaculate. If you are a man, it must be short and well clipped. As the head of one of the UK's largest corporations always said, 'Ears will be worn.' You might like long hair, your friends might rate it very trendy, it might be a positive hit in the discotheque, but in the boardroom it is a solecism. For women, hair can be long, but it must be well cut, as opposed to well styled. At the end of the day, it will look as immaculate as it did at the start because the hair is kept in place, not by glues, sprays or gels, but by each section being cut with care and technique. I know this is not cheap, but it cannot be skimped.

One word of warning. Do not go to the hairdresser just before attending the interview: go two days in advance. They always take longer than anticipated; the hair has a tendency to be unsettled if severe pruning has taken place, and the last thing you need are itchy bits inside your collar or dress in a hot room with an interviewer challenging your right to success. Lastly, your hair must be fresh, clean and free from unsightly grease, dandruff or offensive odour. It must be your crowning glory, and this can apply equally to men as to women.

At the other extremity are your shoes. These must be chosen with the greatest of care. They must match both your clothes and other accessories. Gentlemen, if you must wear a belt with your suit, then make sure the colour matches your shoes. Ladies will automatically make a choice of handbag that coordinates with shoes but men are notorious in this respect. Believe it or not, they think such detail does not matter. They demand to be accepted for what they are. It is the wrong attitude when job-hunting, and is one of the major reasons for prolonged unemployment of the over-fifties. Their reluctance to change, to fit their present surroundings, will ensure that their career stays on the scrap-heap.

If your chosen shoes need repairing, then get it done. Plan in advance. It is no good taking them out of the wardrobe on the day of the interview, to find the heels have worn down or the laces are frayed. Prepare in plenty of time. Do you think I need to tell applicants about clean shoes? You would not believe the number of people who turn up at the interview with shoes that haven't seen polish in their lives. If they cannot pay attention to what should be a regular detail, how are they going to convince the interviewer that they can look after his business?

Now let us look at the bit in the middle of the line. Frankly, sex sells products, but it doesn't secure jobs of any worth. Remember the eye looking for somewhere to settle without causing embarrassment. If a woman's mode of dress is overtly sexual, the interviewer will be in an invidious position. Nobody can comfortably talk to another for an hour or more and never take their gaze from the other person's face. If the only alternative to staring at the ceiling is a bra-less body in a see-through dress, the candidate will be outside the door in minutes. Dress sensibly and carefully. Visit the area where you intend to work. Watch the people leaving the building. Aim to put your dress sense slightly above their level. Go for conservative elegance, good quality materials and subtle accessories.

Gentlemen, watch that tie. A striped tie does *not* go well with a striped shirt. The shirt colours least likely to offend and give the most businesslike impression are white, blue or one of the very narrow pin-stripe patterns stocked by most leading outfitters in grey, blue or red. The suit should be black, grey or blue. An occasional brown is acceptable but risky. The colour to stay away from must be green. No suit was ever made in green that was suitable for business.

Once you have made your choice of clothes for interview, make sure that you have at least three changes. You cannot go to subsequent interviews in the same clothes unless there have been two interviews in between. If you do not have the clothes at the moment, then visit one of the reasonably priced chains and open a budget account. This is called investing in the business. Every company invests for its future, and you must do the same. Do not worry unduly. The investment will repay itself many times over in a very short space of time.

Regarding jewellery in business of a serious nature, this is left to the ladies. Men do not wear sovereign rings, large gold-coloured bracelets and necklaces. If you do not wish to give up these adornments, then get a job in show business, or one of the more dubious direct-selling operations. The serious world of big business is not for you.

Do you look your age?

The age of a candidate is a ticklish subject. The numerous reasons for an employer putting age levels in his advertisements include the cost of health and pension schemes to the company, as well as the consideration of lost time due to ill health. Also to be taken into account is the theory that one's receptiveness to training and the assimilation of technical facts declines after passing the age of forty. It is also not unknown for people in their mid years to display a marked resistance to change in their methods of working. To complete the task envisaged, the candidate may need to possess a marked degree of physical stamina, as well as an erect presence commanding respect, rather than the hang-dog, slumped-shouldered appearance of a man bowed by the pressures of business life.

The first meeting might be with a personnel consultant or a senior member of the company. Unless he is a highly trained personnel manager or consultant, the first impression will sway him enormously. In just five seconds, you have to stamp your authority on the meeting, but you will have very little opportunity to do this with words.

It is estimated that five seconds is the average time a candidate has between the interviewer first seeing him or her through an opening door, and being able to reply to a greeting or make one. Two things will have registered with the interviewer in that time: your appearance, and the way in which you enter the room. If you are older than the desired age range, he will know it from your CV. The fact that he has agreed to see you at all will mean that he is prepared to skip the question of age if it is not noticeable in your demeanour. There lies the answer. When you enter the room, your step must be buoyant, your shoulders back, your head erect. Not only will this make you look young, alive and forceful, it will also conceal a flaccid neck and double chin. The eyes should be intense rather than rheumy. If you wear spectacles, they should glisten, but leave the dark lenses at home or in the car. Project a youthful image from your personality and carriage, not your clothes, and age will never be a problem to you.

Would you employ you?

This is one of the vital questions. You must be brutally honest and put yourself in the place of the interviewer. Look at yourself in a full-length mirror. Go to a shop if you have not got one in the house. Study yourself and ask the question. On appearance alone, would I employ myself? Do I portray the image my prospective employer seeks to give? Could I be described as a suitable ambassador for my new company? If the answer to all of those is 'yes', you can go to the next step. If not, then draw up a plan of change. Isolate your weak spots and do something about them. Visit your doctor if you suffer from acne. Lose a few pounds if your clothes tug and pull and you cannot afford better fitting ones.

Strive at all times for perfection in appearance. You will not achieve it, but you will be so far in front of the opposition that it will not matter. Do not forget the golden rule: a slovenly appearance denotes a slovenly worker. It rarely has an exception.

Your voice

A word on accents is probably appropriate here. I am not convinced that the lack of a cultured speaking voice does not have a detrimental effect on a candidate's chances with some interviewers. Put another way, given the choice between a classic voice and a regional one, some interviewers will plump for the safe bet, knowing that it will be acceptable everywhere. Much as most of industry deplores this, it does still happen on occasions. If you have a strongly defined regional accent, of importance to the vast majority of interviewers is that you will be clearly understood both in person and on the telephone. The simple trick of not trying to assume a classic tone, but remembering always to speak just a little more slowly and a touch more deeply than normal, will ensure that you do not miss the last letters off words. Most people do not speak badly from choice. English is a rapid language that lends itself to corruption. Slowing it down will purify the speech; speaking in a lower tone will give importance to your words. The result will be enhancement of speech, and one more notch on the scoreboard.

Are you shy?

This is a tough subject for those of us who suffer from shyness. Some interviewers will make allowances for shyness in certain circumstances, but it is rare. The sort of position you are going for will generally involve communicating with new people all the time and a display of shyness will be to your disadvantage. Can it be cured? Oh, yes. That is not the problem. With shy people, the problem is getting started.

How to overcome shyness

First of all, let us define the real problem. People are not shy, they are frightened. They are frightened of the unknown. Any person who does not understand something or someone, fears them, even though that fear may be unjustified. If the fear is displayed to the conscious mind, the human will either run from it or attack it. It is as simple as that. Nature has equipped us to attack with great success every time, but while our fear stays hidden in the mind, suppressed by a resistance to acknowledge and do something about it, these tools cannot be used. When we are denying that the fear exists, then we are said to be shy.

What are we afraid of? In the vast majority of cases of shyness, it is lack of acceptance by others. We suffer from a slight inferiority complex. We worry about making fools of ourselves and we do not want to be subjected to ridicule. That, in a nutshell, is the problem.

The way to overcome shyness is first to accept that we are afraid. Once fear is exposed, it starts to melt away. Second, we must examine whether our fears are justified. We quickly discover that they are not. Look around you. Conversations are going on all around us every day: each is listening with varying degrees of attentiveness to the other, waiting to be heard as they put their points in turn. Why shouldn't we join in? They all seem to be having fun, communicating with each other.

How do we start? Let us take the worst case of all and begin at the point where we have difficulty even speaking to others. Start with a smile. Smile at five old people every day. Why old? Simply because this will give no problems or invite trouble to a shy person, which would increase the very fear we are trying to eradicate. Smile at them for a week. The next week, say 'Hello' to five old people every day. On the third week increase this to as many as you meet. The very shy can double the helloing periods to two weeks and four weeks respectively. The result will be the same. Whenever one takes a step, however small, to conquer fear, a part of that fear will be eaten away. Every morning when you arise, say out loud, 'Today I am going to say hello to five new people. This is going to be very exciting and enjoyable.' Repeat it three or four times and inject fervour into your voice. Before you know it, this positive thought will grow into your subconscious, eradicating still more of the fear within.

By the time your interview arrives, you will have gained the confidence to look your interviewer in the eye, say 'Good morning,' and be ready to face the test.

Enthusiasm is the key

All these little tasks that you are being set are designed to achieve one target: to start a fire of enthusiasm in you that will grow as we fan the flames together until it becomes a raging inferno. When I first took to the road as a businessman, 20 or more years ago, I was shy, inexperienced, gauche and naive. I had only one thing going for me: I was enthusiastic. I believed, in my innocence, everything I was told. Fortunately, one of the first messages I absorbed was that success comes not by wishing, but by hard work bravely done. The trouble was that I was forever sailing into uncharted waters. To say I experienced fear was not to understate the fact. There came a time when I needed to develop a system for building up my enthusiasm for impossible tasks.

Calling one day on a company that I would sooner have avoided, given the chance, I parked next to a much older man and got out of the car. As I did so, I saw him take a newspaper from the boot of his car, roll it tightly, and begin to beat it against the side of the roof. Shreds of paper flew in all directions as he hissed venomously with each blow, 'Kill, kill, kill.' After a dozen blows, the paper lay in tatters at his feet. He stared at me with an intensity I have never seen repeated in any man, and said, 'Today, the bastard will give me an order.' Grabbing his briefcase, he strode into the building and was gone.

Sensing that my life was about to change, I waited for his return. I had to wait nearly an hour. When the man came out, I knew he had got what he wanted. I asked the obvious question and he, God bless him, put up with the curiosity of a junior salesman and showed me a signed order for his products worth £150,000.

The newspaper? That was his method of rejuvenating enthusiasm, and I have copied it to this day. It has never failed me and it will never fail you.

Checklist

1. Develop a positive mental attitude.
2. Start to believe in yourself.
3. Get excited at the prospects confronting you.
4. Accept the new ideas you will meet without question.
5. Behave as if you have already got the job.
6. Buy something especially for the first day in your new job.
7. DO IT NOW!
8. Look like a business man or woman, and you will be accepted as one.
9. Inject youth into your demeanour to combat physical age.
10. Use the programme to overcome shyness.
11. Develop an unshakeable enthusiasm for all you do.

Chapter 4

Ready for Combat

Before any competitive situation can arise or conflict of interest take place, certain ground rules must be laid down and a fixed procedure adhered to. If this is not done, no conclusion will be reached. The very existence of these precise definitions provides you with your best weapon. Knowing the rules, one can formulate strategy to overcome the problems set by them. As the whole procedure is conducted in stages, it is possible to attack one item at a time, measure your success, regroup if necessary, and recognize the conclusive engagement when it comes. Now is the right time to study these rules.

The rules of war

The first and most important rule for any sort of combat applies here: know your enemy. In part, this problem will be solved already because of your deep and precise study of the company you will eventually approach, a study so minute in detail that no point or fact will be missed. This is of vital importance. Far too many applicants still approach prospective employers knowing nothing of that company's interests, its areas of trading or its customers, and this ignorance is painfully obvious.

The second rule concerns forbidden weapons. Get this straight from the start, there are none. You are fighting the campaign of your life. Not only do you have the difficult task of convincing complete strangers of your present and future worth, but you have to overcome, if the job be worth having at all, extremely strong competition possibly from both inside and outside the organization. Many companies do more than pay lip-service to their policy of promoting from within. At the very least they are dealing with a known quantity, but on occasions the fact that the candidate is known by the present staff, and either disliked or held in less than high regard, will give your application just that extra chance of success. Do not worry, therefore, when you know the post has been advertised internally.

The third rule is surprise. Be an individual. Be different. Take the company by surprise with your approach to the job, your enthusiasm, your knowledge of the business, your already formulated plans to be implemented when your post is confirmed.

The fourth rule is determination and the need to have it in abundance. Nobody said that getting a superior job was easy. If it were, the job would not be worth the effort. For real satisfaction, one would have to aim higher. The point to bear in mind is that the rewards exceed the effort. Determination is the key. When the keeper throws a large piece of meat into the lion's den, more than one lion goes for the feast, but only one takes the prize. You must be the determined lion. Sink your teeth into the opportunity, hang on fearlessly and defend against all comers.

The job-search path from the employer's angle

With the exception of positions that arise from creative job-search schemes implemented by oneself, the appearance of a vacancy to which one replies has followed a very clear-cut pattern. This pattern has been set in motion by one of a number of events. (1) Perhaps the last incumbent has died, retired, left, been promoted or fired. (2) The second chain involves the creation of a new department, with a lack of in-house staff suited to fill it, no one whom the new head likes, no one who likes the new head, a belief that outside help will do a better job, or that tempting away the better talent working for the opposition will kill two birds with one stone. (3) Expansion takes care of the third most frequent reason to hire new staff, for many of the reasons attached to chain two.

The best position to go for in this group is, in fact, chain two. In the first, there are too many possibilities of getting bogged down behind a head who will neither give up the reins of command, nor allow anyone to overtake him. In the last, the other characters are already established. It may be due to their efforts that new staff are needed to take care of increased business far in excess of existing targets.

You need a position in the second chain which provides the opportunity to show the world what you can do, unhampered by previous example. It has the advantage of being in at the sharp end, tied to operating under the senior management microscope. Your mistakes will not be missed but your successes will be magnified.

So the boss needs a new man. The first question raised at the monthly product meeting is, 'Where do we find him?'; the next is, 'Do we know anybody?'

The latter is a dicey one to answer because if the head puts a name in the picture and the newcomer is a failure, his reputation could be forfeit. How many people do you know that you would bet your job against? The next statement will be on the lines of, 'How did we get Harry in Marketing? He turned out a winner.'

The options here are fourfold:

'He already worked for us.'
'He came recommended from upstairs.'
'We advertised in the local/national paper/trade magazine.'
'We gave the job to Acme Personnel Selection.'

This last is very important. Selection agencies are not cheap. If they can come up with more than one winner for a company on two separate occasions, the chances are that the company will continue to use the SA for the foreseeable future. That they do a good job, in the main, goes without question. It is worth repeating that the cost of replacing a new member of the company shortly after engagement can run to twice the yearly salary, so mistakes are not looked on too kindly. They are only two reasons for the upsurge in personnel consultancies; there are many others.

Whether the company appoints a consultant or not, one of two things will happen. Either the candidate will be headhunted within the trade, in which case, unless you are already down as a high-flier on somebody's list, you will never hear of the post, or the vacancy will become the subject of an advertisement in one journal or another.

The split now is simple. If a consultant is appointed, his job is to present likely candidates to the company. Only in rare cases is the brief so specific as to request only one name. Also rare is the position where the consultant will advertise, interview, test and select until only a couple of people remain. In reality, it is always a mixture. The consultant will advertise, talk on the telephone, interview, weed out, perhaps interview again, then recommend to the employer. At this stage, he may have checked background, personality, various other aspects, but this will depend on the consultant's technique. The most important point, though, will be the chemistry.

The current buzz-word in personnel consultancy, chemistry is what the whole thing is about. Every system under the sun has been tried to find reliable top-performing staff, but at the end of the day, you have to work together successfully. Most skills can be taught to a willing and able pupil, but if he or she is a thorn in the side of the present team, success will never be had at any price.

Chemistry, then, is what they are all looking for. If you can discover the present or new team personality, and fit to it, the job is yours. Is this discovery hard to achieve? Not a bit of it.

Why will he bring in a personnel consultant?

The reasons are simple. The search for staff is very time-consuming: it is precisely because the management have no time that they are looking to increase staff. Picking good staff takes skill in technique and talent in spotting it in others: management are belatedly realizing that not everyone makes a good talent spotter. Personnel consultants can bring experience, contacts and a hard-won reputation to bear. It is no secret that some consultancies attract the best applicants because of the reputation for good positions, fair treatment, and professionalism that they enjoy, while others struggle to get even a reasonable number of replies to their advertisements. Lastly, if the choice is a failure, no one but the consultancy is to blame, and the exercise can be written off against tax.

It is time for another golden rule: always ask the consultant what type of person he is looking for. We shall deal with how to handle this in Chapter 8, but start putting the thought into your mind now, for it is most important, and you have a lot to remember.

Leaving aside the headhunter approach to candidates, which is inappropriate at this stage, we shall concentrate on the most used method of getting staff: advertising. Whether the advertisement has been placed by a consultant or the company itself is immaterial at this point. We are looking only for an advertisement that will fill certain parameters that we can respond to positively, and advertisements of this quality are placed by companies and consultants alike.

Let us assume that you have now isolated the type of job you want to do and qualified this choice with both your personality profile and job description. If you are still unsure, go back to Chapter 1 and start again.

For the purpose of this book, we shall choose the job of Marketing Executive. Apart from giving continuity, it is probable that the majority of readers will be interested in this area, and have a grounding or some sort of experience, however slight, in one of the areas covered by marketing, be it research, sales, or distribution.

Marketing is a very broad brush, however. We need to narrow it down somewhat, so we shall pick another commonly known area within that discipline: the distribution chain. For the benefit of the uninitiated, a word of explanation at this point is necessary.

When a product is manufactured, it is in response to a call from Marketing to provide a product of a particular design formulated by Research and Development, at a price designated by Marketing, to meet a need identified by Marketing (research). Once that product has been manufactured, it must be taken and made available to the prospective customer in the most efficient way possible with regard to time and cost-effectiveness as well as consumer service back-up. This distribution chain is also designed by Marketing as part of its function to identify a market need, suggest a product to fill the need, bring that product to the market, and ensure that the market is aware of its existence and the wish to possess the product is created. The last step in the chain is to ensure that the market can obtain the product as easily as possible.

This is where the Marketing Executive comes in. He is the link between the manufacturer and the customer. However, a simple sales job, calling on village shops selling fast-moving sweets, while very laudable, is not the sort of post we are talking about here, although I must stress that this book will serve you admirably if you are currently working in some dead-end job and see a position on the first rung of the sales ladder as a way to the top in your career. If this is you, hang on tight and hold your breath. You are in for a hell of a ride, and I guarantee you a better job than that.

For this book, though, we shall pick a post of great importance that is well within the reach of any determined marketing man who aspires to greater things. Our guinea pig will be the field link between his manufacturing employer and the distributor, but we are not about to make it easy for him. Let's take away his distribution network, give him a new, totally untried product and place the job with one of the top 10 largest companies in the UK. His responsibility is to create and establish a brand new national distribution network, within the parameters laid down by company policy. He has six months to do it and, from day one, the pressure will be on. How is that for a challenge? Big enough for you? Will we find our man?

In Chapter 2, we decided first that the newspaper and trade journals were going to be most fruitful for this task. Second, for a job of this importance, where the cost of getting the right man will be immaterial, we can expect to find a consultancy handling the initial search. It is not, in fact, quite at the headhunting level, but it would not be unusual to find that the manager who will be our man's boss initiated such a move.

To generalize even further, we shall put our job-hunter – we'll call him George – in an even more difficult position. We shall take him away from a lifelong environment, where a brief search of the relevant trade journal would offer him a number of suitable posts for which to apply safely. We shall not give him any strong background discipline at all. Again, this is probably much like the majority of cases, so whatever your background, this book is going to bring you success.

George, however, knows, as does everybody at his level, that certain papers will provide him with a surfeit of opportunity.

A phone call to his newsagent will ensure that each day he gets the *Daily Telegraph*, *The Times*, the *Guardian*, and the *Sunday Times*. No money? No newsagent? Go to the library. Read them all for free. A day or so either way for a position of this nature is not important. A consultant never closes his list on a particular job until the company has finalized the appointment, and will always find time to talk to another promising applicant, even if it is only for three minutes on the phone.

What do we know about George?

For the job, he is the wrong age group. The company – we shall call them UK Ltd, a branch of UK plc – asked for someone 29 to 35. George is nearly 40. He is married (most of us are at that age) with children approaching O levels, so George doesn't want to move house and take them out of school at a crucial time. UK Ltd wants someone to relocate near to the factory. George is not strong on a single-track career path. He has worked in various products. Some would say that he has had a job or so too many. He didn't go to university, either. UK Ltd wanted someone with experience of their markets, and as they are in a high-tech industry, an engineering degree would have been useful.

UK Ltd and George haven't even met, yet things are looking bad.

UK Ltd take the first step. They commission XYZ Consultants to find a man. They have used XYZ before on two occasions. Each time they have been provided with top-rate personnel, but they have always made the final decision after being presented with a shortlist. This is the well travelled route they decide to walk once more.

The UK Market Manager draws up a job specification, okays it with Personnel to make sure that the salary and benefits are in accordance with company policy, discusses the finer points with his Sales Manager, to whom the new person will report, then passes the brief to the consultant. Human nature then takes over.

Our consultant, having already placed staff with UK Ltd, is beside himself with joy. A third contract must mean that he is doing something right, and he decides that this time he will find the finest available if it kills him. By setting the standards so high, this does not mean that George's chances of getting the job – of whose existence he is still ignorant – are even worse. Not a bit of it. George is the man in Chapter 1: he knows the rules and how to play. They will be like lambs to the slaughter.

XYZ Consultants are experts in advertisement formulation. They know how much truly worth-while staff despise ads that promise the earth and deliver nothing. They realize that to get the best, one must appeal first to the readers' curiosity. They already have good jobs, good salaries, good benefits. First attract their attention, whet their appetite, get them into the office and sell them the job. Hang on a minute – do you mean that the consultants are desperate to get the right man, that once they find him, they will do anything to get him confirmed in the position? But of course. How could you imagine it was any other way? The unsuitable are discarded at the first cut. Do not worry about that fate. That will not happen to you. The rest are put down for interview. Shine at the interview and . . . but I am going too fast. Suffice it to say that you now understand why you should never fear the consultant. He is as desperate as you are to get the right man in the job.

How to analyse and react to an advertisement

XYZ Consultants are given a brief from the company. This they study in great detail. To ensure that the person UK Ltd are looking for matches exactly the type of applicant XYZ are going to attract, key words in the company's brief are transferred to the advertisement. If the company have specified a self-starter, you can be sure those words will appear.

Eventually, the advertisement is written and the copy passed to the media chosen by XYZ. One of these is the *Sunday Times*. A week later, not until the afternoon, George sees the advertisement.

Why did he see it? What attracted him? George was simply following a pattern he had set himself. He made it a task, never to be skimped or missed, to read the situations vacant pages in his weekend paper. He was looking not for good jobs – after all, the pages are full to bursting with those – but for good jobs advertised with sufficient clarity that they gave him a chance to hook his talents on to their pegs from the very start. Let us view an example.

A major international company requires for the UK and export markets,

MARKETING EXECUTIVES

to launch a revolutionary electronic business aid into an industrial environment. In return, a package of £20K plus car is envisaged.

The successful applicants will be required to establish a distribution chain, progress orders employing liaison, negotiation and presentation skills to achieve target, and ensure the establishment of the product.

Call today, on 01-246 8091, to arrange an early interview, or write, enclosing CV, to:

XYZ Consultants Ltd . . .

An exciting prospect indeed. No wonder it caught George's eye. It contains a number of very important hooks, and is one that George has selected for further study. It is here that he employs his analysis technique. Step 1 is the return. Does the package, at first sight, meet the levels he has laid down for himself? An obvious question, one would think, but many an executive has applied for a job that offers a package of X when his financial requirement is at least Y. The reason? He thinks he will be so successful that they will give him a rise in short order, he will be promoted, and the financial question will be solved.

The underlying problem is that this applicant has a subconscious doubt of his own worth. He dare not ask for what he really wants in case of refusal. Had he asked for less, might he have got the job? The answer is always no. No one ever got a worth-while job by offering to work for less than the going rate. If you are not the right choice, you will not get the job if you offer to work for nothing. The moral is, have a high regard for your worth and do not settle for less.

Step 2 concerns the size of the company. Clues here are the spread of operation. The company wants both UK and overseas executives. It wants them simultaneously. The inference is that a chain of command exists to manage executives in both situations. The product is new. It is electronic. It is aimed at the senior executive. It is to be put through a distributor chain rather than sold directly. That sort of product would cost millions to develop, and a great deal to bring to the market-place. A budget of that size, already part spent, denotes again a company of worth. The last clue is the appointment of a personnel consultant who does not skimp on spending.

George is only interested in working for a large company, so the advertisement passes to the next stage of evaluation. What sort of person are they looking for?

Remember George's background. Are any of his weak areas mentioned? Do they want trained engineers? Graduates? Executives of senior manager or director level? It appears not. What is the inference here? They are looking for people who can do what they say, front-ended people who can show that actions speak louder than words. Specialized training can be provided by a company as large as this appears to be. In the first instance, the heading of Marketing Executives appears to mean what it says. The qualification problem for George appears not to exist, so step 3 is out of the way.

Step 4 is looking for pegs. George needs something to hang his application on. The task is to *establish and maintain distributor contacts*. Has George done this before? He doesn't need to go back through his personal profile. That is what he is doing in his present job. An added bonus here – continuity of career. A prospective employer will appreciate this. It is easier to stoke up the fire's embers than start afresh with wet wood.

Progress prospective orders is peg number two. Not only has George solid experience of this activity, he also has his previous experience in an office-based environment to give him a good grounding in the practical side of this. *Liaison, presentations and negotiations* can provide the next peg if it is reworded. Try 'Can you sell from start to finish? To everyone? At board level?'

George has experience of board-level selling. He has also sold to large organizations as well as small. Local authorities, national institutions, all have been subject to his approach. It is all in his personal profile. How about the *achievement of targets*? Do we have a peg here? A check of the profile reveals that George's activity here was up to scratch.

Time for a check. Objective thought at this stage has incalculable worth. Let's go back to Chapter 1 and ask George the first questions. This is his chance to back out if the job is unsatisfactory, or he doesn't measure up, and the time to take it must be now.

Is it the sort of job that George wants? The chance to work for a large company, with good prospects, dealing solely with one link in the marketing chain, launching a product into the UK electronics market, where all the action currently is, would be something George would give his right arm for. The package is good, too, but he will reserve comment on this.

Could he do it? An unqualified 'yes' to this one.

Is he qualified to do it? They do not ask for qualifications. No doubt a degree would impress them, might even be the decider in a close-run fight, but George knows that it will never be that close.

Does he have the experience? A tricky one to answer. In the electronics field, George doesn't know a resistor from a transistor. What he does know, though, is where to get the information. If it was highly technical, the advertisement would have asked for a qualified engineer. It didn't. George decides to bone up on basic electronics by reading at night, and makes a mental note to visit the local bookshop and the public library. A spot of revision on distribution chains and how they are formed will not go amiss either.

The action required suits George even better. He knows that he has a personable telephone manner. It is confident, clear, and impressive. Had it been weak, he may still have applied for the job, but he would then have been one of the second grade, unqualified applicants. Look at it from the viewpoint of XYZ Consultants. They need an outgoing, dynamic personality. They need someone committed to the job. Could it possibly be impractical for the right person to ring on a Sunday? Not on your life. As it happened, over a hundred people rang on that day. Some of those had already got into the running before the postman arrived with initial applications.

Making the call is a terrific way to get over the first hurdle of being considered a qualified prospect for the job but, to the uninitiated, it can also be the fastest way of getting the 'glad eye'. What you say is as important as how you say it, and the objective must always be solely to get the appointment to see the consultant dealing with the job.

What then do XYZ want to hear? A positive, firm voice with a planned attack is vital. This cannot be achieved unless you write down the points you wish to make. The conversation must be structured, it must have progression. You must be in control. If you are fishing for words, it will come over as anything but. Repeating yourself is also another way to dismiss your chances. Reading from notes will get you away from these pitfalls.

What do you write? First your name, address and telephone number, including the dial code and post code. It is hard to believe, but in the heat of battle, little details such as this can slip from the memory or come across indistinctly. Do not leave such silly things to chance. Second, you need to note an extremely short history of your career, relating to the points mentioned in the advertisement. For example, regarding the establishment and maintenance of distribution contacts, when did this happen? How many? Where? Who were you connected with? This is the vital point. Go back for a moment to the subject of corporate identity. If you remember, we talked of using the names of large, impressive companies that we had been associated with, worked with, or, if possible, employed by. This is where they will be most effective, in your opening telephone conversation. You see, the consultant on the other end of the telephone is looking for pegs, too. When George rings, one of the first statements he will hear is, 'Tell me a little about yourself, George.'

At this point, George will give brief statements of his personal situation. He will give his status, ie married or not, how many children, if any. He will say where he lives. Then will come his potted work history. No need to be elaborate. No need to give details such as the full address of his employer and suchlike. The whole purpose is solely to give the impression that George fits the job profile as outlined in the advertisement. This he does by highlighting his activities and linking them to famous names. For instance, let us say that George was involved with servicing a large account for a previous employer whose product was taken by that large account for distribution. George may only have been the smallest link in the chain, but if he says, 'I have been involved in the distribution activity of Household Name Ltd,' the point will have been made and the peg provided. Four or five instances of this type, linking the pegs in the advertisement to previous experience with well-known companies will ensure that George has his closest attention.

It is no understatement to say that, at this time, the consultant will be excited. Without a doubt, he will love his job, and one of the reasons for this is the feeling like no other that he gets when he finds a hot prospect. How many will he get in a day? That is the crux of the matter. There will be precious few indeed, and to get three or four out of a response of 100 calls is fertile soil indeed.

This is the point where, if you are winning, the conversation will change. He will either end it, or give further information about product or company. The most likely is information about the product. What to do if he doesn't give either? *Ask!* This is vital. It is what he is waiting for you to do. Take note, the name of the employer has been omitted from the advertisement. You need it. How will you be able to research the company if you do not know who they are? Likewise with the product. Do not be afraid to ask questions. You must find out what is happening. A word of caution, however. Do not over-play your hand. When you have your information, stop asking. The rest we shall find out in other ways.

Now you need your appointment. You do not need to be a conversational genius to judge the right moment to say, 'The more I talk to you about this product, the more exciting the possibilities become, but I want to know so much more, as you want to know more about me. Are you holding interviews next week, or the week after?'

The consultant's reply will be down one of only two avenues. Either he will refuse you an interview, asking you to send details first, or he will choose either of the offered dates. The latter course, because of the way you have asked the question, is the most likely for him. The salesmen among you will recognize what is called the 'alternative' close. You do not give the person a chance to answer either yes or no. You give two alternatives and he will be likely to choose one of them.

When the appointment date is given, say, 'Terrific. I look forward to meeting you. It will take a little time to put my CV together, so I will bring it with me to the interview if I may.'

Notice that there is no pause, or raising of the voice, when you say '. . . to the interview if I may'. A pause between 'interview' and 'if' gives the consultant a chance to reply. A reply to that statement is the last thing you need right now. You are about to get off the line, and fast. Just thank him, confirm the date, say 'Goodbye' and put down the receiver. If you have reached this stage successfully you now have a 90 per cent chance of getting the job. The rest of this book is about turning that 90 per cent chance into a 99 per cent certainty.

The offensive lies with you

You must realize at this point that it is up to you to make the right impression. How you say things is as important as what you say. If you are in command of what is said, then you will be that much more in command of the outcome. Never forget, the consultant is looking for George to show him that he is worth interviewing. George must show that he has substance, that he is different from the run-of-the-mill applicant. He can only do this to best effect in front of his adversary. To get there, he has to be skilful, devious, and enthusiastic. More than every word written in this chapter, enthusiasm is the key. It must ooze from every pore.

Your face must be aflame when you talk on the phone. People cannot see you then? Rubbish! I can see an enthusiastic man or woman 5000 miles away, and so can you. The more enthusiastic they are, the more I want to meet them. Carry the battle to the enemy, and bash him with enthusiasm. Nothing in the universe can withstand that.

The various battlegrounds and how to choose them

It is important to realize that George's war will be fought on different fields. The first will be the consultant's armchair. He will have around him the CVs of as many people as he has invited to apply. He will also have a number from people who have simply written in on spec. Added to that will be the odd letter from time wasters and cranks. All this activity might be going on at his office desk, the worst battleground of all, where distraction after distraction piles in on his day, breaking his concentration and pulling his mind away from the job at hand. An over-long study of one applicant's CV might end with a brief scan of another as his phone rings for the umpteenth time.

On almost none of those CVs will there be a face. They are just words, creeping over the edge of the page or leaping to his eye, as the case may be. Either way, he has no image to fit them to. How many of you have read a book after seeing the film, in which your favourite star was featured. How vivid then it all becomes. How clear in your mind's eye are the exploits of your hero when you can put a face to the character on the page.

This is the purpose of taking your CV to the interview. Nearly everyone else will have sent theirs in, to compete with each other for attention. You, by choosing your own battleground for this vital exchange, will stand a better chance of firing direct salvos. Not only will it be read at a different time, but its construction will be such that he will want to take it home to read it. This scores two important points. First, he will not be referring to it through the interview, picking bits at random and firing questions at you. Second, he will be able to absorb it in peace and quiet, free from the pressure of knowing he has perhaps two dozen or more to cover before lunch or dinner.

There are, of course, other battles to come. We shall cover them as they arise. Be happy that the first exchange has gone overwhelmingly in your favour.

The compulsory letter approach

While the writer would always recommend that one should only attempt to respond to an advertisement that asks for an initial telephone approach, this is not always practical for a number of reasons. Therefore, we shall deal with this problem of the initial compulsory letter now.

Why do you need to send a letter?

A very large number of executives always keep a prepared general CV in their desks, whether they are job-hunting or not, in case of the sudden arrival of a golden opportunity within their own company or outside. Personnel consultancies know this, indeed they often expect it, and use this fact to help them with the initial weeding out of applicants.

They simply ask the applicant to write in at first instance, and expect him or her to include a CV. They expect the CV to do the talking; any letter accompanying it should just refer to the post advertised and ask for consideration. Long, wordy letters attempting to sell the applicant at this stage are a mistake and could lead to the application being dismissed no matter how good the CV. Reason? The applicant is showing painfully obviously that he does not know the rules of the game.

How to construct an initial letter

The first rule is, always write it in your own handwriting. Make no mistake, this is of vital importance. It is an even money bet that your handwriting will be analysed at this stage. As we have already seen, graphological analysis is a very precise and true indicator and is used by a great number of companies and consultancies.

Do not waste your time by trying to write in a hand totally unfamiliar to you, to give a different impression of your character. This will fool no one. Neither should you get a friend to write it for you. The best results will be obtained by spending time reading about the subject, studying your own hand until you can differentiate between its points and then, if it proves necessary, adjust your hand to eliminate the negative aspects and improve upon the positive. Be sensible about this. Do not try to do too much. Remember the exercise is to bring out your best strengths and give muscle to the weaker ones while playing down unwelcome traits, not to turn you into the personification of moral perfection. No one would believe you if you were.

Always use black or blue ink, never ball point or any other substitute. A nib will improve the weakest of handwriting. Do not use a fine nib. A medium or, even better, a broad nib will give strength and character to your letter and will be easier to manage if you are unfamiliar with the instrument. If this is the case, then practise by copying from a book or newspaper until your words flow freely and you feel at home with the pen.

The paper should be white, A4 size, and of the same quality as the CV, the best you can afford. Never skimp on this detail or diverge from the rule. Your letter will be copied and filed, so it must conform to the accepted business standard and present the right appearance when viewed in duplicated form.

The correct format

After drawing a rough draft and seeing how much space it will take up, start your letter in one of two ways. You can either write your address in one line along the top of the page or in the top right-hand corner. Whichever you choose to suit your personality, make sure that it includes your telephone number and STD code, and that it is legible. Margin your address from the right-hand side if you are using the latter format, leaving plenty of space to get each line in without cramping or getting too close to the right-hand edge of the paper. Punctuate every line properly. Such attention to detail will score valuable points.

Next, and further down on the left-hand side, comes the recipient's address, starting the first line with the name of the company or consultancy. Start at least an inch in from the left-hand side of the paper and this time line it up on the left-hand side. Follow this line down the page whenever you start a new line, and also ensure that your text on each line ends against a similar imaginary margin. You are striving for neatness, precision and attention to detail. Practise until you get it right.

Some advertisements will ask you to address your letter to the Managing Director or some other title. If a name is given, with qualifications after it, always duplicate these exactly. On the next line, put the company's name, followed by the address and the date.

Start your letter 'Dear Sir,' or 'Dear Madam'. If you are replying to a woman do not get into conflict with the 'Ms' style currently in vogue unless it is specifically stated in the advertisement. You will annoy more people than you befriend by being condescending. A woman can be successful without being a feminist. Sign off 'Yours faithfully'.

The actual wording of the letter causes a great deal of worry and confusion, but this should not be. Let us look at the reasons for writing it.

The advertiser has stated that he wants more personnel. He wants you to apply if you truly think you can do the job. He wants you to send the CV so that he can appraise your qualifications for the job and initially assess your suitability. Your aims are the same. That is exactly what you want him to do, with the addition that you want him to invite you to an interview. How do you achieve this? By simply asking, and no more. You refer to the post advertised and ask for consideration. You must not try to sell yourself in the covering letter. This would be overkill and would divert the impact of your CV.

Is there a standard wording? Bear in mind that many thousands of people will read this chapter. Originality will count in your favour, but one or two points must be included. Mentioning the date and name of the publication in which you saw the advertisement will help the advertiser judge response from different journals, and he will mentally thank you for it. It will also give him an idea of your reading preference.

Stating the job applied for will also help. He may have advertised in the same journal on the same day for a totally different post. An ambiguous reply will confuse him and he will discard it.

Do not confuse brevity with a lack of communication skills. The recipient only wants to know why you are writing to him and what you want him to do. This is not your opportunity to show him your skill in essay construction. Your CV will do all that for you.

Bearing in mind previous comments on originality, study this suggestion for an initial letter and check for the above points, then construct your own.

Further to your advertisement in the Daily Telegraph of 22nd February 1985, inviting applications for the position of Marketing Executive with UK Limited, London, I wish to be considered for the post.

I enclose my CV giving full personal and professional details to assist you in this matter, and look forward to hearing from you at your convenience.

Yours faithfully,

Conclusion

Here we have been studying an ideal case. The name of the company has been listed, which is not all that common with consultants, and you have been able to include it in the CV.

What happens if no company is referred to? Your approach must be modified. Your CV can contain no reference to the company and the appropriate headings and references must be omitted. Neither can you include the resumé to the CV that is discussed on pages 73-4, in which you offer to work on a probationary basis, because you do not know, as yet, whether the job will be worth that commitment.

Because of these restrictions to your initial approach, such advertisements asking applicants to write in must be chosen with the greatest of care. Only those with the fullest details must be replied to, to enable your CV to have a complete structure. There is no reason why you should not contact the consultancy by phone and ask which company is seeking staff. They may not always tell you, but you need to know in order to start research. If the information is not forthcoming, then consider whether you ought to apply. Bear in mind that a vague application will lose impact and place you among the masses. It will be that much harder to achieve recognition. A resourceful applicant will always score heavily and create a better first impression which is so vital with this initial letter approach.

A final point covers the reply you hope to receive. Many applicants complain of bad manners on the part of companies because they never write back to candidates to tell them that they have been unsuccessful. Avoid this uncertainty by enclosing a stamped, addressed envelope. The number of applicants to an advertisement is so high nowadays that few organizations can spare the time or money to write back to everyone. Your courtesy will give them the chance and once again score points in your favour.

To summarize, then, always try to find advertisements that do not ask simply for you to write, in the first instance, enclosing a CV, but if you feel you have no option, construct your initial letter with care and brevity and follow the simple rules outlined, making sure that your CV and letter, placed unfolded on top of the CV, are securely but not bulkily packaged. Thick manilla or linen-backed large envelopes are ideal for the purpose and easily obtained from good stationers. Do not skimp on presentation here, and always use first class postage of the correct denomination.

Checklist

1. Learn the rules of war.
2. Apply them.
3. Study and understand the job-search path.
4. Start reading those job ads.
5. Practise ringing for interviews with a friend.
6. Analyse as many ads as you can.
7. Believe in your own worth.
8. Look for pegs.
9. Practise providing them.
10. Qualify the ads with the four steps to success.
11. Write a telephone script.
12. Build up that enthusiasm.

Chapter 5

The Application Form versus the CV

The methods which different companies use to record details of their staff will almost guarantee that, at some time, you will be required to complete an application form. This is not, and never will be, a substitute for a curriculum vitae (CV). It is purely a record for Personnel to hold on file, to be referred to in the future should the need arise.

Why companies use both

It is not unusual to find, after an application has been made for a post, that the company sends a four-page application form with ample space for your qualifications, career details, personal history, and the other dozen and one headings always included. You must fill it in. This is vital. Just as important, you must never treat this form as a substitute for a CV. It has neither the space nor the appearance for that job, and will fail you miserably.

Others will, of course, treat it as such, thereby removing just so many more names from the competition. They are the unenlightened who will never learn.

XYZ Consultants, however, need to know more about you than a simple form can ever portray, and for that they need a complete CV. What is a CV? It may be a list of your past jobs. It will almost certainly be a record of your education and qualifications. It might even mirror your ambitions if you spend just 1 per cent more of your time compiling it than the usual rubbish sent in by the competition. None of these goes far enough, however. What it should be, first and foremost, is a statement of your personality. It should sum up everything you are, and have to offer, for your future employer. He should be able to look at it and conclude, without turning a page, that its subject is diligent, committed and enthusiastic.

A four-sided application form could never do that in a thousand years. Both forms, then, are vital to your progress, and this chapter will tell you how to compose the two to greatest effect.

What to write on the application form

It is important that the CV is always written first, but as that is a lengthy task to describe, we shall return to it later, especially in Chapter 6. Suffice it to say that it is already done, and you can refer to it.

The main point to remember is that exactly the same words must appear in duplicated passages on both the AF and the CV. After filling in your name, address and general details, the first item to pose a problem will possibly be education. List your educational details starting from your school age, to the present day, but do not list anything before the age of eleven unless you are specifically asked to do so, or unless you attended the same school from preparatory years to senior school and beyond. If you had a public school education, then make very sure that that is obvious. Do not rely on the name to see you through. It may be read by an immigrant to this country who knows little of our great institutions. Always put, for example, 'Hardwich Boys Public School' rather than just 'Hardwich School'.

Never attempt to complete an application form in longhand. No matter how hard you try, it will always look scruffy because your writing will differ from the typed headings and instructions, the ink used will differ from the duplicated image and may even clash in colour. Do I need to say that the same applies to CVs? Always type them. If your typing is not up to scratch, get a friend to do it, or give it to an agency. If you are having your typing done elsewhere, make sure that they know exactly how you want it set out, give them examples, and check it diligently for spelling mistakes. You are paying for perfect copy, and have a right to get it. If you see a mistake, get the whole page retyped. Do not allow the use of Tipp-Ex or any other form of eraser.

Most application forms have room for education details, but they sometimes sadly lack anything like enough space for career history. If this is the case, congratulate yourself, and write in the space provided: 'Please refer to attached CV.'

What to miss out

Important details lose their impact if they are crammed into a tiny space allocated by the form designer. He has only so much paper to work with. He is not interested if it affects your chances of getting the job. That is your problem. Do not, therefore, allow his constraints to bully you into spoiling your presentation.

The next important item to miss from the application form, if you are asked for it, is that nebulous passage worded on these lines: 'Please list all reasons why you think you should be considered for the position.'

Your answer is the same: 'Please see attached CV.'

The impression you are giving is that there is insufficient space in which to write your answer. This is always acceptable. The real reason, of course, is that you do not want your details taken out of context or sequence. The whole point of the CV is that it is a selling document. It has a beginning, an affirmation and a close. Read wrongly, the buying desire will not be created or passed to the reader and the effect will be lost.

The importance of the CV

We have already stated the job of the CV. The importance of the document can never be overstated. It will be referred to by your interviewers throughout your series of meetings, it will be written on, highlighted, copied, passed to higher management, studied by various specialists and thrown back at you in the form of questions.

None of this will cause you any problem, however, as the recruiters will all base their actions on the CV, but *you* wrote it. You will know it inside out. It will be a part of you. It is the most valuable tool you have, because the company must use it but *you* have total control over what goes in it.

How to construct a CV with impact

Put yourself for a moment in the shoes of the consultant at XYZ who is conducting the search for personnel.

You have spoken to George on the telephone, been suitably impressed by what you have heard, very pleased that out of the hours you had to stay by the telephone, a handful of likely prospects has appeared. Now you know that when you interview them, not all will be able to go on to the next stage. They just will not be suitable. You will have to do some weeding out. Are you pleased? You are getting nearer to your ultimate choice? Not a bit of it. You are fed up, because the small number of people from whom you had a choice has now been whittled down even further before you even had a chance to balance one against another.

Before the date of the first series of interviews that you have set, the CVs start to come in. When you get them, you read them at your leisure, or hurriedly, as the case may be, and highlight points of interest, items to discuss when you first meet the candidates.

Already you know that you have made a mistake with one or two. Their histories are just not holding up to the early promise of the telephone call. The choice is narrowing . . . what is the next thing that comes to your mind? Of course! *I hope to goodness that George is worth while*.

The moment the consultant thinks that, you have him in your

pocket. He is relying on you to come up with the goods. Now do you see why the CV must have impact? When you get there, and hand it to him personally, it must knock him off his chair. It must leave him speechless. It must make him, for a few minutes at least, forget all the rest. You will have his curiosity aroused before you arrive; the impact of the CV must capitalize on this.

You have to be different

You have already displayed originality in your approach to the telephone call to XYZ Consultants, and in what you have said on that call. Now you must continue with, and enlarge upon, this theme. Your CV must be different. That alone will give it the impact to help you succeed. How different, we are about to discover. This much is for sure, it will require the expenditure of a few pounds, but you must be prepared to invest in your future. If you have no money at all, then wait and save until you have. If you are chasing your first job after university, go and speak to your parents. They will be delighted that they can help. Why not talk to your bank manager? Tell him what you are doing. Show him your draft copy. The bank manager doesn't exist who would fail to be moved to help you when confronted by your enthusiasm.

This is so much a case of the end justifying the means: every effort made towards your goal will repay itself a million times over. How would you feel if you knew that the job could have been yours, if only you had retyped that one page with the mistakes in it? I'm being finicky? Don't you kid yourself. In a matter of such grave importance, nothing can be left to chance. The result is everything.

There are a number of people who specialize in writing CVs for their clients. They do an excellent job, but they are not for you. Never employ a professional. First, all the good ones are known to the personnel consultancy industry and their work is instantly recognizable. It shows lack of originality and will earn you at best a black mark; at worst, your CV, which may have cost you a pretty penny, is consigned to the waste bin. When your interviewer looks you in the eye and asks, 'Is this all your own work?' nothing will keep the pride and enthusiasm out of your voice when you answer in the affirmative, and it will score heavily in your favour. A lie will never be as convincing. Who knows, the one he put down two minutes ago may have been exactly the same as yours. What price originality then?

Fluent writing and how to achieve it

It is obvious that the better writers among you will produce, initially, better CV copy, but that is not a problem.

First you are going to write about yourself, so inspiration, or the lack of it, will not prove a stumbling-block. Second, the time schedule is not so tight. I guarantee that you have nothing better or more important to do, so you can work on writing and re-writing those passages until you are totally happy with them.

Get a second opinion. Put down what you want to say in two or three ways, and take it to a person whose opinion you value. Get them to make suggestions and re-write in your own words. After two or three days of real effort, even the least literate among you (and I mean that in the most kindly way) will be producing flowing prose that reads and scans beautifully. Finally, be scrupulously correct with the punctuation. Your employer is looking for a person with an eye for detail, because he knows that inattention to detail in the long run will cost him money. Display that attention through your punctuation and correct spelling, and the psychological points will keep mounting in your favour.

The 10 pages that will make you a winner

Your CV will be 10 pages long. Sounds a lot? Believe me, you cannot do it in less, and when you see how the pages are constructed, you will wonder how applicants could consider submitting a CV in any other format. Each of these pages has a task. Each will lead the reader along a path from which it will become increasingly difficult to diverge. The ultimate conclusion? You will either be appointed, or passed unequivocably to the next stage of interview with a 'highly recommended' slip attached to your application.

There is one further point to be stressed before we go on to the meat of the CV, dealing with its construction page by page, and that is the difference between honesty and embroidery.

On average, 90 per cent of what you are about to write will never be checked. It is not unknown for 100 per cent of what you write never to be checked, but you cannot afford to take the chance. If, for instance, you claim qualifications that you do not have, and are asked to provide documentary evidence when you start the job, the game will be up and you will be on the street. If you call yourself a National Sales Manager in your last position, and the new boss rings up your previous employer to be told that you were a Representative in control of Devon and Cornwall, you will never be able to repair the damage.

Embroidery is a different matter. If a skilled needlewoman decides to make a new set of cushion covers for the sitting-room, she will still only use simple needles and threads, but she will weave and stitch those threads with such artistry, such painstaking care for detail, that the result will be breathtaking to behold. The moral is simple. A desire for one's services is created by painting word pictures of one's achievements rather than by a grand title. The more artistic the picture, the more likely the chance of success aimed for.

Checklist

There is only one task at the end of this chapter. That is: start to gather information concerning your past history and practise describing it on paper. Remember, we are aiming to list everything in a very concise form, but the basis must be complete before one can start reducing it to fundamentals. You never know, the writing practice might not come amiss either.

Chapter 6

The CV – Page by Page

In this chapter we shall cover every aspect of the CV and its construction as it relates to getting facts down on paper. It is advised that notes are made as we progress, and practice taken on each page until a satisfactory result is obtained before going on to the next. This will encourage the growth of confidence and literary skill.

Type of paper

The final, finished copy of the CV must be on the finest quality paper you can obtain or afford. At the very least, it must be of the standard accepted throughout industry known by the trade name of Conqueror, but go for better and more expensive paper if at all possible. Use only A4 size and make sure that it is white. Colours for this purpose are unacceptable. I have seen CVs produced on different colour papers with matching inks that have attracted me, but the risk is too great. Stick to black on white and you will offend no one. The edge of the paper must be cut straight, not deckle finished. You are writing to industry, not your Auntie Florrie. Type on one side of the paper only. Leave a 2-inch margin on the left of the page and a 1-inch margin on the right. When the paper is in the binder, the script should then centralise. Adjust these figures if necessary, depending on the type of binder you decide on: just make sure that the script is exactly central. Leave at least an inch at the top and bottom of the page.

Binding

The pages of your CV are going to be split up at some time. Copies will be made of them which will eventually be filed and sorted. For this reason, it is impractical to present the CV permanently bound. *Never* ever use a stapler or paper-clips. It is so unprofessional at this level as to be totally unacceptable and inappropriate. Rely on the cover to hold the pages together.

Cover

It is obvious that your CV will need a cover. This cover must look expensive. It will denote to the recipient that the contents are of the greatest importance. If this impression is achieved, then the contents will receive so much more considered and careful attention as to make the whole exercise a total success. Do not skimp on this detail. Search the shops until you are totally satisfied that you have found a binder that will complement the details within. What you are looking for is a very stiff board binder, covered in leather or a very good substitute, with a sprung spine. This type of spine, when the wings of the binder are pulled back, opens to accept pages that do not need holes or perforations, then grips them securely on release. Avoid any type of binder that requires holes to be made in the paper. If any sheets need to be removed for copying, the holes show up and look very shabby. They also tear with heavy use, to the detriment of the CV's appearance.

Various colours are available, but black, wine red or bottle green are least likely to give offence.

Do not expect to get the binder back after presentation, and *never* ask for it. When you hand over your CV, you will make something of an occasion of it. To request the return of the folder would cheapen the moment irrevocably.

The front page

The first page of the CV is always a title page. On it should be simply a description of the contents, your name, the position applied for and the name of the company to whom you are applying. This should be centred on the page as accurately as possible, bearing in mind that a portion of the left-hand edge will be inserted into the binder and therefore be out of sight. An example of the format would be:

Brief of the Qualifications of

GEORGE THOMAS BLOGGS

Applying for the position of

MARKETING EXECUTIVE

to

UK LIMITED

Note the slight offset to the right, also the use of upper case type (capitals). Do not underline; it never looks neat enough.

Nothing else should appear on the first page.

Personal details and your photograph

Page 2 consists of a number of headings dealing with your personal details listed beneath a photograph.

To deal with the photograph first, this is of the utmost importance in registering the right impression. When your CV is shown to other people who have never met you but are being asked to make decisions on your suitability at that stage, it is of the greatest assistance to you that they can build up an affinity by seeing your photograph. It is so true that a picture is worth a thousand words. The personality may send you running for cover, but how many times have you studied a photograph of a person and immediately felt, 'He/she is fabulous. I'd love to meet them!'?

The second point is even more psychological. Not all of us would win prizes in beauty contests. At the first meeting, our appearance might not, to put it kindly, cause much of a ripple. A skilful photograph, however, can do wonders for bringing out our best side, toning up or down a weak or over-strong feature.

Do not settle for a passport photograph taken in a booth. It just will not do. Neither will a holiday snap, nor the one that mother said you always looked so good in.

You must go to a person who knows his job, operates in the industrial field, and understands your needs when you explain them to him. The best people to use are small advertising agencies. First, they will have the professional equipment, with a suitable backdrop of a neutral colour. They will be able to take a series of pictures in different poses, both left side and right as well as full face. It is rare that a full-face shot has a better effect than one where the shoulders are half turned away from the camera, but it is important that you have the chance to study all the angles and pick the best. One single shot is never good enough.

The picture should show just head and shoulders, with the subject dressed in a suit or, if female, a blouse or dress suitable for business use. Do not use a colour photograph. Apart from the expense, a better effect will be obtained for this purpose in monochrome. Colour photographs require special make-up to be effective and may reveal more defects than would be desirable.

The photograph should be 3½ inches wide by 4 inches deep and mounted on the top half of the page with the personal details below. Use a good quality adhesive and apply it sparingly; too much will show through to the face of the photograph and spoil the whole effect.

The details underneath should follow a series of headings as in the following example:

Name:
Address:
Telephone: (Include the national code.)
Date of birth: (Write out the month completely, do not
               abbreviate.)
Status: (Married or single. Do not write divorced or
               separated.)
Children: (List numbers, sex and ages.)
Health: (If you can honestly write 'Excellent', then do
               so. If not, then enter 'Good'. If disabled in
               some way, omit the section completely, but
               make sure you are fully capable of carrying
               out the required workload.)

Education

Details of your education will comprise the third page of the CV. These must be broken down into four sections.

1. First must be listed the schools which you attended from the age of eleven onwards.

   The major examinations taken and passed, such as Common Entrance and scholarship exams, must be included as well as subjects taken at O and A level. Never claim a pass at any level if none was attained. This is vital. Many employers, after giving you the job, will ask for certificates to verify your claims, especially in a technical capacity. If you sat for the exam, fine. Then say so. If you failed, there is no obligation to inform anyone of the fact.

   Also in the first section should be details of your university career, if you have one, with all relevant dates and degrees attained.
2. The second section should list educational and professional qualifications. If these are minimal, do not emphasize the deficiency by spotlighting it: add the qualifications to section one.
3. The third section should list the various extra-curricular school and college activities in which you took part, with pointed reference to such items as debating societies, literary and chess clubs and computer studies groups. Any other activity with a business leaning should be mentioned but being a founder member of the Badge and Bangle Club is hardly going to influence a prospective employer, so be selective.
4. The last section should deal with your sports achievements, listing years in which you represented your school or house. Evidence of the ability to function as part of a team is of vital importance.

Career history

Depending on the breadth of your work experience, this section, starting on the fourth page of the CV, could well run to two, three or even four pages. The reason, of course, is content. It is important not to boast, brag or lie, but there is no reason to be ashamed of achievement. If it takes three pages to list your career in a proper, businesslike fashion, then so be it.

The information needed is worthy of deep study. The impression you are trying to get across is one of gradual advancement along a carefully chosen career path. Not everyone, however, starts out along the same trail that they finish on, so a move into another discipline is not a black mark against you. As long as you give the reason for the change, it will be understood.

Another problem can be caused by redundancy. People have found themselves leaving two or three companies in succession due to redundancies, but giving this as a reason for changing jobs more than once does nothing for your career, even though the fault be not of your making. Cruel, I know, but there it is. Far better to state the reason for the department closing, intimating that the reason for your leaving the company was the event described, not that you were singled out for redundancy. A fine point? Perhaps, but an important one, and remember, you did not tell a lie.

Career history, then, should start with your first job upon leaving school, and progress through to the present. It is not necessary to list the full address and telephone number of each employer. Just their name and the town location will be sufficient. Also, a brief description of what they do. Stick to one or two words. For instance, if they were involved in making widgets and gizmos for the construction of off-shore oil installations, 'Petrochemical Engineers' is quite sufficient. Should the company be a household name, then just a one- or two-word heading to describe the divisional activity is sufficient.

After putting down the date of starting and leaving, and the name and location of the employer, with a description of his business, we come to the most difficult part, that of listing your position and describing your activity. Let us first quantify what you are trying to achieve.

You need to get across to your prospective employer that you held down a worth-while position, but when you were young you would have been expected to start at the bottom. Do not be afraid therefore of stating this. It is not, in the first few years after leaving school, *where* you join a company that is of major concern. What is important is, what did you learn? Also, what greater responsibility was placed upon you in how short a time? Did you leave a better job than you joined? Were you seconded to another department with increased workload? Were you taken up as a senior person's assistant?

Do you see the point? You must be able to demonstrate progression and capability. Your position must, therefore, be listed, with a brief description of your responsibilities and to whom you reported. Next must be listed any training of a formal nature supplied by the company, such as sales courses, technical seminars, but omit general tuition received in the general course of events. Highlight any training relevant to the job for which you are applying.

You must list any and all activity relevant to your new post. This is most important. What you are seeking to achieve is a rapport between the reader and your career history. He will be impressed by evidence you give of success with projects and tasks for past employers, but he will be ecstatic if he finds that your greatest successes seem to lie in the areas for which you are being considered. It is extremely difficult to give examples of this, but it will help if you are reminded to use words and phrases to describe your performance that have first been used in the original advertisement. Go for this association all the time. The vital watchword is *relate*. Whenever possible, make your career path and working history relate to the advertisement.

Lastly, at the end of each job description, you must give a reason for leaving. Consider these reasons most carefully. Remember that the prospective employer may well contact an old employer for a reference. If you are considering joining a secure department in the civil service, the armed forces or the security services, you can almost guarantee that they will wish to confirm a few facts at least. General industry, however, can vary. Strange though it may seem, many references are not taken up for many reasons, some of them quite valid. The point is, if you have a skeleton in your cupboard, now is crunch time. Do you mention it?

My advice is . . . no. Of course, I am not referring to the habitual criminal. Such people have no place in business as they are often far too unreliable. Occasionally one comes across a different case, where a stupid mistake, instantly regretted, has cost the person dearly, and he is either bent on restoring his life to a proper basis, or has done so and wishes the days to speed past, in an effort to put as much distance between then and now, as fast as possible. As regards criminal activity, the Rehabilitation of Offenders Act gives certain guidelines and lays down set periods after which offences no longer need be mentioned. A telephone call to your lawyer will give you chapter and verse on your particular crime and cost you nothing. For the others among you who have been sacked for bad work, laziness or misconduct, then creative writing and faith in your particular God are the only weapons at your disposal.

Do not attract attention to a bad work history by leaving big chunks of the past out of your CV. Your new employer is unlikely to take up a reference more than five years old anyway. Keep the dates on which you were employed by each company as accurate as possible.

If you have chosen to leave a company, and it wasn't two steps before they fired you, there is nothing wrong in a month's break between employers. I have often seen CVs giving breaks of longer duration, even a year, where the applicant has been engaged and references never checked! Have faith in people's belief in human nature.

Reason for applying

What your prospective employer will be interested to know, however, is why you want to leave your present position, or why you already have. This must go on the last page of the career history, and be headed: REASON FOR APPLYING FOR POSITION WITH UK LTD.

When concerned persons read a CV, they nearly always have a bright yellow or green highlighter pencil in one hand, with which they mark relevant passages for re-reading later. This is one passage that you can guarantee will get the highlighter treatment: it makes a positive statement about your application, and will play an active part in securing the post for you. It must, therefore, be constructed with the greatest care.

It must be brief, three or four lines at the most. It must have impact, to drive into the subconscious and stay there. It must be sincere and believable. It must *link positively* to the advertisement. Again, how do you give guidelines to every reader to cover every job possibility? The task is impossible, but to construct an example for George is not so hard. Perhaps you will study this, in the light of the job he is trying to win, and find inspiration.

After a great deal of thought, rewriting, and more thinking, George wrote: 'I would like to concentrate, and bring all my energies to bear, on the one function that I find totally absorbing and challenging, that of being the link between the manufacturer and the chain of distribution.'

Will it help him to get the job? We shall see.

Specific experience

All the experience you have received in various jobs is of interest to a prospective employer, but what he is most eager to discover is the experience that you have gained in the fields relevant to the job for which you are applying. This is one of the most important pages in the CV, therefore, and must be the result of a great deal of thought.

Without specific experience, you may well be an excellent executive whom any company would be delighted to employ, but not in that position. This is where we must go back over our notes and search for the items of relevance. In George's case, only dealings with distributors can count as specific experience, so they must be isolated and emphasized.

The skill lies in making the utmost of your experience. It is not enough merely to say that you were involved in distribution. You must develop facts, give figures and point up your success. You must use the knowledge gained from the telephone call to the advertiser to assess what areas you will be working in, what level of responsibility is required, what expansion of the job is likely, what customers you will be dealing with, and build the page around that knowledge.

Lastly, you must have at least three paragraphs but not more than four. The appearance of the presentation is all important, and more than four paragraphs of five or six lines will give an overrunning problem. By keeping all the relevant information on each heading to no more than one page, apart from the career history, you enable the reader to turn a page, deal with a subject to his complete satisfaction, then turn again to a new subject knowing that he has all the facts without disturbing the concise continuity.

Training background

The position for which George is applying is concerned with the setting up of a distribution chain, but let us make no mistake, when he goes into the field, he will be required to sell. Why? Simply because people buy people, not products.

If he cannot sell himself to the prospective distributor, he will be unable to sell his product, and sell his product he must. He must convince his prospect that (a) he has the right product at the right time in the right sector of the market at the right price and (b) the after-sales service will be second to none and the marketing support likewise. To do this, he must be able to sell.

The prospective employer, therefore, is going to ask what sales training George has received. Again, it is not enough merely to list the courses in order of attendance. That tells nothing. The important point is what was gained from the courses: what techniques were learned, which are being applied at present, and why.

These must then be tied to the task in hand and a recommendation given as to the most suitable techniques to solve the forthcoming problems. An explanation must be included as to why only those, in your opinion, will be successful.

The importance of this is obvious. If he agrees with you, your statement carries double weight. If no one else writes of such a technique, then you score for originality, you display considerable depth of mind and enthusiasm by showing in a practical way that you have made a serious attempt to study and analyse the problems ahead, and you are one more step nearer attaining your goal.

If you achieve nothing at all because your future employer disagrees with your concept, he will at least acknowledge that you have an opinion and are not afraid to state it. This implies the power to make a decision, which is not a bad impression to leave any businessman with.

Relevant qualifications

Ask yourself a simple question. Who is the person most likely to get the job? Answer? The man who can offer most. It is as plain and straightforward as that.

All through this process of getting the job you want, you are showing that you are prepared to go to any lengths and offer more than your competitor to secure it. When it comes to qualifications, this is where you really play a trump card.

You have already listed your academic qualifications, but if that was all the employer was looking for, he would not have got to this page of your CV. Why? Because there is always someone who is better qualified academically than you. They will always have a better degree, a more comprehensive list of A levels, and so on. If that was all that was needed, the employer would have scoured the appropriate universities and looked no further. He requires you to have a reasonable and applicable level of intelligence, to be sure, but he needs something more, something relevant. When George leaves the office for the first time and enters the jungle outside the door, his employer wants to feel secure in the knowledge that George is qualified to handle himself in hazardous encounters. For that he needs more than a degree in engineering or an A level in history. He needs relevant qualifications.

It is worth noting here that this is the section where the person with very little in the way of academic qualifications starts to make up ground.

What is a qualification? Nothing but proof that certain qualities exist in the person, whether they be put there by training of the mind or personality development.

Personality, then, is what we are dealing with here. To complete this page, we need five short paragraphs of two or three lines each that will deal with the five most important aspects of personality:

- A track record of success.
- A broad depth of experience in the relevant field.
- A developed sense of self-reliance and persistence.
- The ability to work under pressure, in a team, with targets, and be able to achieve them.
- The physical presence to command attention and respect.

Each of the headings must be expanded upon within each paragraph to get over conclusively the impression that these qualities exist in the applicant. If that is not achieved, then the CV will not be a success, and the application may fail.

Again I shall list five model answers, but you must take the greatest care in formulating your own and not copy the passages word for word. Remember, you are not the only reader of this book!

Track record

A track record in selling and marketing products closely related to the field of operation involved, and experience of launching a new range of products into distributors.

Experience

A broad depth of experience in selling to distributors and customers of the status and breadth likely to be encountered in the position.

Developed sense

The possession of a developed sense of self-reliance and persistence to follow prospective orders through to a satisfactory conclusion.

Work ability

The ability to work under pressure, to function as a team member within a chain of command, to accept the imposition of sales and order input targets and to achieve them consistently.

Physical presence

The age and physical presence to command the attention of decision makers and achieve the objective of negotiating, presenting and liaising with them.

Let us review what has been done here. Reading the list, we discover that George is qualified in a relevant way by past activity. He has experience of just such a task as that which he will be set. He has the ability to broaden his scope and deal with bigger situations. He has guts, determination and enthusiasm. He is not a maverick, accepts authority, works well with it and others and understands that everything achieved is usually a team effort. He knows all about targets and views them without fear, confident that he can meet them and confident that they will be fairly set. He is, lastly, the sort of man that gets things done. He is a leader, an inspirer and one who earns respect, not demands it.

Be honest, even if he had no formal qualification at all, wouldn't you want to meet him? Of course you would, and that is all that George is asking; the chance to present his case face to face.

A point of importance to note, however: idle boasting has no place in a CV. The points above must be put across with humility as well as firmness: 'May I propose the following as being relevant qualifications for the position that I seek.'

Resumé

What does it all mean? What does the reader feel when he comes to the end of your CV? Have you done enough? Is there still the possibility that a final statement is needed? After all, you have not just listed the qualities and qualifications that suit you to the job. You have presented a case. You have listed the objectives and objections, you have almost talked to the reader on an informal basis. Does it need another page?

I think it does. At the end of every report, there is always a summary. When an advocate defends his client, he does not rest on the evidence and the impressions given to the jury from the witness box. He gathers together the facts and presents them in such a way as to try and leave the jury with no doubt of his client's innocence. This is the time for radical ideas: the time, if the case hangs in the balance, for putting new thoughts in the minds of people who may well be sceptical.

George's task is no less difficult or crucial. He knows that mistakes made at this time by the employer will be extremely costly. He wants to secure a position from which he can further develop his application but allow the employer to walk away without burning his fingers if all should not turn out as expected. How can he do this?

He offers a trial. He states his case, sums up the reasons for it, and makes the radical proposal that they employ him on a trial basis. He suggests a probationary period.

The psychology behind this is simple. If he gets the job, his contract of employment will state that a trial period will be in force for the first three months. This is standard but not always plainly stated. The most common clause used is, 'The employment will be subject to one month's notice for the first three months, thereafter two months' notice from the employer and one month from the employee . . . '. The inference is obvious. If one does not come up to expectations, one is out, with the minimum of fuss within the law.

George has gone one better. He has said, 'Give me the job. If I fail, I will walk away there and then, and make no claim upon you.'

What does the employer have to lose? Nothing. Furthermore, every time this technique has been used, to my knowledge, the employer

73

has never taken up the offer. He has always confirmed the employment in the normal way and the applicant's job has been secure. The point is, the applicant has been prepared to 'put his money where his mouth is'; the employer has recognized this, and scored the person that much more highly because of it.

Sincerity is paramount, though. To say it, you must mean it. That cannot be stressed too highly. Do not make offers you are not prepared to back up.

Salary

Throughout the CV, no mention has been made by George of the salary he would expect for the position. He knows what the scale is from the advertisement. Had it not been mentioned, however, he would now be facing a dilemma. Should he ask the salary, in case it is insufficient for his needs, and risk appearing mercenary and interested only in the personal rewards, or should he accept what is finally offered with good grace and hope for a pay rise in the near future?

The answer is . . . neither. There is a time and place for the salary question, and it is most definitely not in the CV. Rest assured that at some stage in the interview sequence, the package on offer will be outlined. This will usually come in the interview with Personnel, but does arise in other interviews depending on the size of the company and who is making the decisions. Various rules apply here, and they bear study.

First, if you are applying solely for the salary, stop wasting everybody's time. You will never be successful in the post and should not ask for it. You are however, a saleable commodity, and worthy of your hire. If you are applying for a team position, one of a number of people taken on board to do the same job, then the salary scale will already have been decided and any changes highly unlikely. If you are moving into an existing team, to replace a person who has left, for instance, the same rule will apply. Negotiation will only come into it if the job is a 'one off'. Here the rules of the game are very different.

Every employer knows that by paying peanuts, he will end up with monkeys. He is not, however, there to make you rich at his expense. He will have a rough idea what he is prepared to pay, and what supplementary benefits he will attach to the post. It is up to you to negotiate and try to achieve the highest price. Good negotiating practice does not start with you quoting a price in your CV. Neither does it start with a premature statement at interview of how much you think you are worth. You must wait until a figure has been suggested to you. Only then do you consider the question of reward. If at all possible, your reply is not given at that time.

Let us assume that the advertisement for the post stated that the salary was negotiable. This is your first indication that you will, at some time, enter a bargaining situation. A general scale will be mentioned to you at some point, along the lines of, 'and your salary will be negotiable in the management scale for the job, Mr Brown, which is currently £20,000 to £25,500. This is up for review at the moment.'

They always say the salary is up for review. This is to stop you asking for more than £25,500, on the grounds that you will get a rise in the near future. Of course you might, but I would not advise you to hold your breath while you wait. In practice, unless it is written into your contract, the bargaining is done, the terms agreed, you start, and your details go into a file. A rise will come after you have proved you can do the job, and then some, or you are promoted. The last is unlikely considering you have just been employed to perform a specific task.

The reply to the salary question, then, is a simple 'overcoming the objection' sales technique statement.

'I can understand your asking about my thoughts on salary, Mr Smith, but before I can make any informed decisions, I need to know more about the job I will be doing, and you certainly need to know more about me. Tell me, would I be correct in thinking that . . . ?'

Follow up with an intelligent question, and steer the conversation away from money. This method will rarely fail, but if it does, and the interviewer is persistent to the point of asking again, be firm. Do not allow yourself to be forced into making a statement at an inopportune time. It will damage your prospects of a higher salary and give the impression that your negotiating skills are weak. If he can shut you down with a simple question, once repeated, how are you going to get on with a tough prospective customer who tells you that he sees no need for your product or service? You are not applying for a job in sales? Learn a good lesson, and never forget it. All business is selling and everyone sells.

When you judge that the time is right, and salary must be dealt with, the initiative lies with you. The best time is when you have been offered the job. If you can wait until then, you have won the battle handsomely. Why? Obviously, he would not offer the post without agreeing salary unless he was agreeable to paying any price within reason. Few indeed are the jobs lost because a negotiable salary could not be agreed after the job was offered.

The opening in both situations is the same: 'I am sure you would agree with me, Mr Smith, that the time is right to discuss salary?'

If it is not, he will tell you so, saving you the embarrassment of making a bad decision. If he agrees, and you must wait for him to agree verbally, not just charge in without getting his affirmation, your statement will have concentrated his mind on the closing question. Further, you are closing the sale of yourself to his company by removing the final objection. You are now only seconds away from the most important question of all, but we shall leave that until much later. First things first.

You have his agreement to discuss. Do not plunge in with a statement that gives him no reason to accept it. The most common mistake is to say, 'I have been considering a figure of £26,750.'

His mental response will be, 'Have you, indeed? And what makes you think you are worth that much?' And a perfectly natural response it is, too. You have to show him first what he is getting. You must stress the benefits and get him to agree every one.

'Now, for whatever figure we finally agree on, you will require me to do . . . ? I shall also be expected to employ my experience on setting up a . . . ?'

And so on, until your major strengths have been itemized. At the end of each statement, include a phrase on the lines of, 'Is that not so?' or, 'That is correct, isn't it?' To be certain of getting your points across, you must get his affirmation each time.

'I am sure you would agree with me that those tasks and responsibilities are worth at least a package of £27,000 pa, Mr Smith, wouldn't you?'

You have achieved two major points at this stage. He knows where your thinking is placed, and you have given him the chance to strike a deal. He has room to manoeuvre should his board flatly refuse to sanction any amount over £25,500. The operative word is package. He will either agree, or state his price. If he is bargaining, be firm. Do not drop the package figure but convert a small portion to reward in kind, for instance, a better pension, an extra week's holiday, a higher value car. Do not, however, be intransigent. Keep your finger on the pulse by asking questions and guard against overplaying your hand.

Wouldn't you rather deal with successful people?

The point of all this negotiation is to achieve position and respect with your superiors. If they have had to pay a high price, they will value their acquisition that much more highly. They will expect more, of course, but you are prepared to give that anyway. People will always choose to deal with successful people if humanly possible, and if you start with success under your belt, your upward progress will be that much more easily achieved.

Checklist

1. Do not settle for the first draft of any statement that you make. Revise and reconstruct until you are truly happy that you have achieved perfection.
2. Concentrate on originality of thought and statement. To succeed, you must stand out. To do this, you must be different.
3. This task of constructing a CV cannot be done in five minutes in front of the television. Accord it the importance it deserves and reserve a special time for it when you can work unhurriedly and alone.

Chapter 7

How to Get the First Interview off the Ground

We have now reached the crux of the exercise. You are about to meet your interviewer for the first time, and he or she will most likely be a personnel consultant for an agency employed by the company. The same rules still apply if the first interview is a meeting with the prospective employer.

Making a friend on the telephone

We have already dealt with the initial telephone call, but it is worth stressing here that the impression you left must be sufficient to engender true curiosity. If you spoke comfortably to him, established a rapport, gave him an inkling of your worth, he will be looking forward to meeting you. Why? You can almost guarantee that the people he has seen already will have been, in the main, a waste of time. When he sees your name on the appointment schedule, he will remember, and his heart will lift. You will not disappoint him. You will have made a friend on the phone.

Make him come to the door

How many people, I wonder, have to start interviews by being led along corridors to the interviewer's office by the secretary, only to walk into the room and be confronted by a head bent over a desk? This is often a ploy to unsettle the applicant, or it may be genuine, but that is not the point. If he is truly interested he will come out and greet you personally, or he will find an excuse to come to the outer office to give himself a chance to look at you, to gain the psychological ascendancy (although he may not realize it, that is exactly what is happening).

If your first contact makes him come to the door, then score a big point. Be assured, interviewers will not do it for everyone. How you react will reduce or strengthen that position, but we are going too fast. Let's get you to the office first.

The importance to morale of minor incidents

Getting a job, even when you are as well prepared as you will ever be, is a stressful, harrowing experience. Tests have shown that the heart-beat can rise to a staggering degree, on a level with that experienced when a serious accident has been miraculously avoided while driving. It is important to do your utmost to settle the stress and avoid damage to morale, therefore. You must take every step to ensure you are as calm and in control as possible. Let us imagine that our friend George has his interview today, and see what he has done to prepare.

A pre-interview action list

The night before, George stayed at home. He didn't go to the pub, neither did he over-indulge at his favourite restaurant. He didn't spend the evening preparing for the next day, either. That would have been too late if something had gone wrong. His suit came back from the cleaners two days ago, and has had a chance to hang and air. All the papers he will need have been assembled in his briefcase, including two spare pens, a pencil, an A4 scratch pad, two copies of his CV, all the information he has on his prospective employer and any correspondence that he has exchanged including copies of any letters he has sent.

Tucked in the back will be six sheets of kitchen roll, half a dozen safety pins, a packet of elastic plasters and a spare tie. A lady will also include two pairs of tights or stockings and sanitary protection. If a train or plane ticket is required, then that also will have been purchased two or three days in advance. Finally, never forget a road map showing clearly the location of the office you are to attend. George will be driving down, so he has already rung the receptionist, told her that he is coming for an interview in a few days, and enquired about parking facilities. There are none, so he will use the nearest public car park. The office is in the centre of London, parking is scarce and expensive, so George will allow £5 for this. His appointment is at eleven o'clock. An allowance of two hours to travel 60 miles means he will arrive at nine thirty. Why? Because something will always go wrong if you leave things to chance. How can you possibly rely on 55 million people doing exactly the right thing at the right time to enable you to get to your appointment punctually? Don't risk it. Give yourself a spare hour and a half at the very least. More, if you can.

At nine thirty, George is driving past the office. He knows the location, he knows now how to get there from the car park and roughly how long it will take him. He has also seen a café 100 yards away in which he can relax and prepare his mind. As he leaves the car park, it starts to rain. George's preparation has given him time to wait in shelter for 10 minutes until the shower has passed. As he hits the pavement, he looks a million dollars, but what is more important, he feels it.

George is aware of a problem he suffers from, and one that is fairly common. Under stress, in a warm atmosphere, he sweats. No anti-perspirant exists that can safely and inconspicuously be applied to the brow with total effectiveness. Again, planning ahead, he arrives at the office 15 minutes early. After introducing himself to the receptionist, he immediately asks to be shown the lavatory. This stops the receptionist from ringing straight through and precipitating an early meeting with his interviewer. Don't forget, the previous applicant may not have shown up, leaving a gap in the schedule.

In the comfort and privacy of the wash room, he can remove his jacket, wash his hands and face, give a buff to his shoes and fine-tune himself mentally. With seven minutes to go, he is back in reception, being asked to take a seat. With a pleasant and laughing, 'Thank you very much, but I spend far too much time sitting down,' he declines the offer. He also declines the offer of a cup of coffee. Neither does he smoke. On a table is a selection of magazines. He chooses *Punch*, displaying a sense of humour, rather than a business magazine, which is too pretentious, and opens it. He does not read it, simply scans, keeping his senses alert and his eyes watchful. If the interview is on the company's premises and a house newspaper or product brochure is available, he will read that. He will also ask the receptionist if he may keep it. He will scan it rapidly for details of relevance to his position or points of interest that he can use for an opening statement.

It is important not to be seen doing nothing. More than one company has the interviewer's wife working in reception and her impression will be eagerly sought on your departure. To sink into a low chair, and bury yourself pretentiously in the *Financial Times* is to court danger. You will crease your clothes, appear self-important, and put yourself at a massive positional disadvantage should your interviewer suddenly appear and introduce himself. There are ways to extricate yourself from this predicament, but it is better if you do not get stuck in the first place. The time for sitting is later on.

Hotel interviews present an unreal situation, and fortunately are being used less and less these days, with the increasing ease of travel, but should you be required to attend an interview in one, the same rules apply. How are you to know the identity of the man at the next table who is watching you with obvious interest? A stranger? Your new boss?

The importance of the receptionist

Whether from nerves or an inflated ego, some men can never resist the chance to chat up a pretty girl. In this situation, you do so at your peril. Be pleasant, smile a lot, but be the soul of propriety, and do not stare at her body every time she walks past you. Office staff discuss this sort of thing in front of their superiors. You are there on business: let's keep it that way. Her job is to help you. She will give you every piece of information you have a right to ask, and will do her best to see that you are comfortable and happy. She will be the one to inform your interviewer that you have arrived. Make sure that she has done it, and score another point if your attitude has put a cheerful tone in her voice.

It is not likely that you will be kept waiting, but if it happens, be patient, and refrain from asking every five minutes if the interviewer has forgotten you. Show calmness and relaxation of mind. If after half an hour you have still not been shown in, then say to the receptionist, 'Do you think they might have forgotten me, or is he with somebody?'. This must be said without antagonism, but not without a slightly serious note attached to it. That will elicit a serious reply and put your mind at ease.

Five seconds to change your life

When the interviewer comes to greet you, you will know it. He will have a sense of purpose about him, and will look you straight in the eye as he approaches. He will probably smile and extend a hand. Give it a firm one-two shake and release it. That is all. All other types of handshake are dangerous at this point. Never offer your hand first. Some people have an aversion to shaking hands and if he ignores you you will feel foolish and rejected. From the moment your eyes meet, lock them on to his and do not let go. Your face must display cheerfulness, open-mindedness and enthusiasm. He will invite you to follow him to his office. Say, 'Thank you very much,' and then put the magazine down. By leaving the disposal of the magazine until after the greeting, you will display that you are happy in your environment, confident in the ability to make decisions in your own time, and have a chance to break eye contact legitimately.

Five seconds have passed, and impressions have been formed. If it all went smoothly and to plan, you are out of the traps and on the race of your life. What is more, you are in front.

How to recover if you muff it

The car wouldn't start, the motorway was blocked, the car parks were full, you hadn't any change for the ticket, you lost your way, you got soaked in the rain and you trapped your finger in the revolving door. As you introduced yourself to the receptionist, with not a minute to spare, your interviewer walked out of the office and said, 'Hello, Mr Brown, would you like to come through?'

Above all, do not panic. You need five minutes to recover, and you must get it. The only way you can do this is to ask.

'Excuse me, Mr Smith, but if you could give me just two minutes . . . ?' Leave the question hanging, but do not sit. Your manner must be of one who will be deferred to. That two minutes is vital to your composure and you must get it. When you return, apologize for the delay, but do not cringe. Treat it as a fact of life, an obstacle that you successfully overcame, and you can turn defeat to victory. One can sympathize with another if factors beyond one's control go awry, but apologizing implies that one accepts responsibility. It is then looked on as one's own fault. The rule is, never apologize.

Putting it in perspective

It is not unusual for a new person to be given responsibility for the fate of a product that was developed at a cost of £5 million, allocated a budget of £1 million for advertising and product awareness, and £2 million for the marketing function. That is a lot of responsibility.

As we have already said, changing personnel soon after appointment can cost twice the salary package.

Hidden costs include the loss of credibility and reputation of the person who did the hiring. This can be incalculable and could result in a ruined career.

In view of the potential consequences, allow for subjective reactions. Put yourself in their place for a moment: you have interviewed, run test programmes, interviewed again, checked references and consulted colleagues. You still feel uneasy? That is chemistry at work. A successful, practised interviewer will know within 10 minutes of first meeting a candidate if he is the right man. Skills can be taught. Company attitude can be implanted. Basic chemistry can never be changed, and you must be always aware of this.

Are you exerting influence?

Have you exerted any influence over the outcome at this point? Most certainly. Your telephone conversation, your appearance, your punctuality, your enthusiasm, your pre-approach investigation of all aspects of the company and the post have put you in a strong position. This position is so commanding that *you* are now about to take control of events. There is a long way to go, but it is all downhill. Prepare yourself for one of the bumpiest but most exhilarating rides of your life. Believe me, the result will be worth every bruise and scratch.

Expenses – who pays them?

Every company worth its salt will pay interview expenses incurred by the applicant, but not all personnel consultancies do. If money is tight, you need reimbursement and it has not been mentioned, then ask. When dealing with the company, the Personnel interview is the one at which to raise such questions. With the consultancy, this question is asked when you are about to rise to your feet at the end of the interview. A simple question on the lines of, 'Have any arrangements been made to reimburse travel expenses?' is quite sufficient. It is important that you do not appear as a financial midget. There is nothing wrong in expecting reimbursement but if it appears to be the most important thing in your life at that time you will be downgraded in the interviewer's eyes and suffer a heavy setback. To ask if any arrangements have been made rather than to say, 'Am I going to get my travel costs back?' reduces the question to a simple one of company policy, and gives the impression that the answer, be it negative or positive, affects you not at all.

Checklist

1. Practise your telephone technique by ringing for jobs that you do not want. This will build confidence and remove careless errors of speech and approach that could be most damaging if left undiscovered.
2. Study your material, CV, and background information until you are word-perfect. The more that is etched into the memory, the more time you will have to consider questions carefully before answering, and the more complete your answers will be.

Chapter 8

The First Interview –
an Exchange of Ideas

This part of the first interview is where you establish what is wanted from a successful candidate. It is also where you will start scoring points, and you must be aware of this. Some interviewers have a habit of making notes but this practice is not as widespread as it used to be. If it happens with you, ignore it. You cannot see what is being written, and as likely as not he is noting good points rather than bad, so be encouraged and do not let it put you off. Make an effort, if he is writing, to give him time to do so. He will thank you for your consideration. If you can see what is put, and he appears to be writing your statements for later use, then talk at dictation speed with your head angled and your eyes on the pad he is using. He will then know that you are perspicacious enough to spot his needs and chalk up a point in your favour.

Affirmation and scoring points

In any situation where you are selling yourself, be it a presentation to a customer, your colleagues or senior management, or being interviewed for a job, the practice of affirmation is the most important part.

It is a proven fact that a person will only remember 10 per cent of what he reads, 20 per cent of what he hears, 30 per cent of what he sees and 50 per cent of what he both sees and hears. To increase that awareness, one needs to reaffirm one's points. This must be done in a firm way, but not with arrogance. 'Have I explained that fully to your satisfaction?' is better than, 'You do see that, don't you?'

If you are asked to explain how you would perform a certain task, then do so in clear concise terms, affirming each important point as you make it, and rounding off with the above question. When you ask that question, say and do nothing more. Give the interviewer time to answer, and do not proceed until he does. Each time he does, score one point. The more points you score, the better you can judge the success of the interview. Do not forget to score against yourself if you make a mistake. Without a balance, you will not get a true reading.

A word on mistakes. If you are asked a question and you muff it, perhaps by answering too quickly, do not let the situation lie there, with a point against you. Always say, 'Let me just restate that point. What I am really saying is . . . '. Score a point for making yourself clear and another for turning the situation around. Your interviewer will be nothing less than impressed. Be aware. Going home in the car is not the time to say to yourself, 'I wish I had dealt with that question more effectively.' The opportunity has gone, you have left the interviewer with the wrong impression, and you may have made a fatal mistake. Correct errors as they occur.

Conducting the interview

It is as well to list, at this point, certain verbal skills that will help you in making your case. Study them and apply them. They are very important.

1. Be human. Don't sound like a tape recorder.
2. Do not be a preacher or orator. Keep a conversational style.
3. Do not apologize and never make an excuse.
4. Always look at the interviewer and maintain eye contact.
5. Avoid prepared jokes. Keep humour spontaneous if the context is appropriate.

A word on point 4: not everyone likes to have eyes boring into theirs constantly. It can be off-putting. It is acceptable to drop one's eyes momentarily but the situation to avoid is where, for example, you give a complete answer to a question never taking your eyes from the picture on the wall. If you find looking into a person's eyes difficult then use a psychological trick. Look at the bridge of his nose exactly between his eyes. Because of the human focus, he cannot tell that you are not looking at his eyes, but you will find it very comfortable and easy to maintain.

More useful points to remember

1. Use conversational English, not prose.
2. Avoid impersonal language. 'I tend to think that . . . ' is better than, 'It is considered that . . . '.
3. Use abstract terms as little as possible. 'At this moment in time . . . ' has so much less impact than 'Now'.
4. Keep it simple.
5. Do not use words like meaningful, ongoing, scenario.
6. Avoid repetitive phrases. Ask a friend if you have any.
7. Do not be predictable or your audience will switch off. Verbal surprises keep them awake and alert.
8. Do not over-use the technique of rhetorical questions.

9. Narrative is important. A collection of facts in a story will have impact.
10. Do not be negative. Which sounds better?
'We cannot solve this problem by increasing staff because . . .'.
or
'The obvious way to solve the problem is by increasing staff. Unfortunately, it will not work. Let me tell you why . . .'.
11. Do not be afraid to use notes, or to refer to them.
12. Never read from a prepared script.
13. Physical mannerisms like scratching one's nose are less irritating than repeating, 'You know', or 'As I say' three times in every sentence. Better still, don't do either.
14. If you are nervous, do not worry. It will not count against you.
15. Pause between phrases. A stream of words is boring and hard to take in.
16. Do not be arrogant or boastful.

Visual aids

If you can present any facts in a visual form, then do so. Make copies and take the greatest care over their production. Make doubly sure the figures are right. Take copies. When you have given the interviewer a copy, then explain, looking at yours, what it is all about and what you are trying to show. When you have explained, go over the benefits related to your chart or figures, reaffirm to get his agreement that he understands and agrees, and then go on to the next subject.

Make your mark

Although, in the first instance, the interviewer will be leading the conversation, you will have a couple of minutes to establish yourself and break the ice. It is here that you have an opportunity to make your mark, and it comes in two sections.

First, the ice-breaker. If you are a natural conversationalist, this will pose no great problem, but do not start until he has settled. We shall assume that he has met you at the door of his office or in reception. Either way, he is still standing. You have greeted each other and exchanged pleasantries and you are on the threshold of his office. If he shows you into the room, go first. Do not stand on ceremony or display false modesty. Let the entry appear natural, with you at ease and in command. If he is behind you, do not attempt to close the door. Leave it to him. If you are shown to the office by another person and the door is opened for you, as it should be, enter firmly, but not hurriedly, and pause on the threshold for a second. Fix your eyes on his and approach the desk smiling. Do not lower your gaze. He will probably rise and extend a hand. Shake it with a firm grasp, twice, and take a chair only when he sits or indicates that you should do so. Remember, if no hand is offered, do not offer yours.

If there are a number of chairs in the room, pick one slightly to the side of his desk and not too far away. If no chair is in a suitable position, then move one. This will show that you have fixed ideas of your own, and that you are not prepared to suffer an uncomfortable position. Do not sit in a hot window or by a radiator.

When you are shown into a room, do not attend to the door yourself, but leave it to the secretary. If you are alone, and the interviewer remains seated, close the door behind you in your pause period by pushing it behind your back with one hand. On no account must you lose eye contact as you enter the room.

Position and the power struggle

You are face to face, the ice-breaker has opened up the situation, and it is time to establish your position and gain ascendancy in the ensuing power struggle. How do you achieve this? With the first of your trump cards. This is when you hand him your CV.

Visualize the scene. You are both seated, he has had a chance to note your appearance and get used to your face. This is important. People need this break for adjustment to feel easy about you. All the signals flashing across between both of you are at this time purely on the subconscious level but are no less important for that. Once that situation has run out of steam, he will be ready to pounce. You forestall him by saying that you have your CV for him.

What a surprise! He will be expecting the usual two or three sheets of sometimes folded and dog-eared paper, when out of your case you will bring this leather-bound folder which you handle with reverence, almost with awe, and pass to him only when you have also taken out your copy and closed your case. Do not just hand it to him. Make a presentation out of it. The higher regard you afford to the document, the higher the esteem in which he will hold it.

As he starts to look through it, say nothing. Just watch his reactions. I promise you, he will be impressed. The chances are he will put it to one side with the care that you displayed when you gave it to him, accompanied with a comment like, 'I will have to sit down and read this tonight.'

Now, the whole battle is open before you. You are at your high spot, and it is up to you to capitalize on it. You must start off with the first question: 'Obviously, Mr Smith, I have conducted a great deal of research into both the position and the company since speaking to you, but it would help enormously if we could begin by talking about the responsibilities of the post. How do you see my area of operation?'

You are in. The contest has begun. From now on, your concentration must not waver for a second. At every question you must think before you answer. You must speak firmly and authoritatively, as a person who knows his subject. You must concentrate on proving that you possess the qualities referred to in the advertisement. That, after all, is what he is looking for. All the rest is verbal fencing, an irrelevance.

Once you judge that the interview is coming to an end, certain questions must be asked, but do not let that end come without taking some company literature from your bag to let him know that you have truly researched the company, using any visuals you have brought, or asking questions.

Do not rely on natural inventiveness when it comes to question time. It will fail you. Have your questions listed on an A4 pad, and make sure that there are at least 10 of them. Do not ask a question if the point has already been covered. That is why you will need at least 10.

Salesmanship is what it is all about

Very few orders were ever obtained without the salesman closing the sale, and it is no less true here. How do you close a sale? You start by restating and emphasizing the benefits to the purchaser, then ask for the order. Nothing could be simpler. If there is an objection, you deal with that, affirm that the purchaser is satisfied, then go for the close again. Got it? Let us see how it works in this context. Referring to your notes, either imaginary or real (and I would suggest that they be real) you reaffirm the benefits by stating the points raised in the advertisement and subsequent conversation.

'To clarify my thinking, Mr Smith, the sort of person you will ultimately choose will be able to demonstrate a high degree of business acumen?'

'Most definitely, yes.'

'Fine. And he will also need to have had contact with . . . ?'

'That is true.'

'Third, you are looking for someone who can show determination?'

'Most important, that is.'

'And also self-reliance?'

'That too.' And so on.

Do not list more than about six features, but make them all telling ones, highlighting your greatest strengths, including experience and qualifications if you have them.

You then get in for the close:

'Tell me, Mr Smith, do you have any reservations about my suitability?'

If he says 'Yes,' ask him what those reservations are. You will need the answers to work on before your next interview.

When you have the reservations spelt out for you, ask, 'Do you feel any of those points are a barrier to my proceeding to the next level of interview?'

He will undoubtedly say, 'No.' Had they been, you wouldn't have got this far.

Your final question is:

'That is terrific, Mr Smith. Now, how do we proceed to the next step?'

'We shall be sending you a letter in the next two weeks, outlining the procedure and . . . '.

That is when you get up, thank him for his time and for giving you the opportunity to sit and discuss what is, for you, a tremendously exciting position, or words to that effect, but note the points made there. You have thanked him personally, you have registered your pleasure at being considered for interview, and you have restated your *enthusiasm* for the position.

If his answer was 'No' to your first closing question, then proceed to the final one with even more enthusiasm than before.

Body language and its importance

Try as we may, we can never prevent our bodies revealing our true feelings about a person or subject, even though our mouths may be saying something entirely different. You need to know what these silent signals are and how to interpret them. It is important to recognize that one signal does not make up the whole picture. Two or three signals need to be taken together to give an accurate diagnosis.

For example, your interviewer may say: 'I am prepared to listen with an open mind to anything you have to say.' At that point, he stretches out his legs and crosses them at the ankle. First pointer, but could be meaningless. He might just have pins and needles in his knees. However, he also crosses his arms over his body. A warning sounds in your brain. Third, he leans back in his chair and looks at the ceiling. The message is obvious. Don't confuse me with the facts, fella, my mind's made up!

Consider another situation. You are explaining a point to him and he says, 'I see that quite clearly.' Does he? Is he leaning forward with one elbow on the desk, looking downwards, and rubbing the back of his neck with his hand? He doesn't understand at all. He is confused, and you know it.

As you talk to him, his ankles come uncrossed, his hands rest in his lap or on the desk in front of him. He then leans forward. He may be sounding cold and unconvinced at that point, but you have his uninterrupted attention. Assume the same position yourself and you will know you have established a splendid rapport.

Beware the finger rubbing the nose or eye and the dropped gaze as he speaks to you. He is quite possibly lying to you. Look for this when he tells you he will be contacting you in the near future with a view to further interview. If you see it, ask him if there is any point before you leave that requires clarification. You might just get out the big objection before all is lost.

This subject is too comprehensive to deal with here, but I stress the importance of it most highly, and recommend you to read one of the excellent books available on the subject. You will find it entertaining and enlightening and it will certainly be an asset to you when being interviewed, as well as in everyday conversations.

How to drink your coffee

There are a number of loose ends that need tying up at this stage, and they are all important although individually insignificant.

You will probably be asked if you would like a coffee. On this occasion it is right to accept. It is a psychological gift. To refuse will affect his subconscious adversely. When you get it, let it cool before attempting to drink, then consume only half to two-thirds of the cup. Do not drink it all at once. This way, you have shown acceptance of his friendly gesture, pleasure in the gift, and a practicality of mind. Would you like a biscuit? No, thank you. This is an area fraught with danger. What if they are soft, sticky chocolate ones? Keep out of trouble. Would you like to smoke? Have one of these? Not on your life. The most dangerous thing to accept at interview.

Just for fun, I once offered a cigarette to interviewees on a recruitment programme, waited until they had accepted one, then said that I didn't use them myself. The expressions ranged from sadness to panic. I had also removed all ashtrays from the room! One chap artfully rolled the ash down his trouser leg to collect in his turnup, disposing of the stub in his handkerchief. Resourceful indeed! Amazingly, only one person out of six asked for an ashtray. I don't care how badly you need a cigarette, don't light up at interview.

What we are talking about is stress. The interviewer will try one or two ways to see how you perform under stress, so the less chance you give him, the more obvious will his efforts become. You might even get the paper-clip question. 'How many ways can you think of using a paper-clip, apart from holding paper together?'

Don't laugh, I have had that question asked of me on more than one occasion. Be prepared.

Overcoming objections

Quite simply, if you cannot overcome his objections, how can he expect you to overcome the customers' objections? Did he just raise a serious question? More to the point, did you allow him to? That is the whole point about objections. You must know your weaknesses in the situation as they relate to getting the job, and you must bring up those weaknesses in a casual manner and dispose of them before they loom large in his mind. It is not difficult to do this. Just make sure that when you do raise a question, you have the words to go on and state the positive side to get it out of his mind. Never forget, you know what your weaknesses are – he doesn't.

Sales aids – what to take and when to use them

We have already mentioned visual aids in the context of graphs, charts and lists. Their use can relate either to your past experience in handling a similar situation to the one you are applying for, or to how you will do the job once you get it, and the performance you can achieve.

Applicants for sales positions can use charts to show how they will get effective coverage of their area and achieve targets.

Other sales aids to secure the post include all possible publications available on the prospective employer. Write to the head of Public Relations and get a company report as well as details of the product on which you will be working. Ring the sales office and ask for details. Test their organization at the same time. It all comes under the heading of company research, and that is one thing that you cannot have enough of. If possible, speak to an employee. Discover the names of the people you will be working with. Another effective aid you can bring out is a company chain-of-command tree. Introduce it and ask where you will be on the tree. This sort of preparation is absolutely invaluable.

A final word on research. Make sure it is accurate. You will not score many points for talking about a product that was withdrawn six months ago. Get it right.

Finally, check your activity between application and interview. Were you busy with not a moment to spare? You were? That is good, but you probably still didn't do enough. The moment you get home after the interview, start digging further. You need new facts, and you may not have much time.

To round off the interview, you must send a letter to the interviewer. This letter must give your thanks for the interview, stress how pleased you were with the outcome, how you look forward to meeting the interviewer again, and how your enthusiasm for the job has been heightened further by what you have learnt about it. Lastly, get it in the post that very night. Promptness is everything, and such a letter carries enormous weight. It could be the last little thing to tip the scales in your favour against the competition.

Is there any competition?

It is always helpful to find out if you are the only hot prospect, and one of the surest ways to do this is to ask. He will not be offended. He will expect you to want to know what your chances of success are. The possibility of a vague reply is high, but if your luck is in, and you have created a good rapport, he may say, 'Well, we do have two others to choose from at this time, but do not worry, I am pretty sure we will be able to put your application forward to the company.'

For what more could you ask?

How to leave the building

How many applicants have lost the chance of employment because they walked out without saying 'Goodbye' to the receptionist or secretary? It is difficult to guess, but I do know that the vast majority of interviewers always come out of the office and say to their staff, 'What did you think of him?' A bad impression left by the applicant will lead to a non-committal reply, or worse. Don't take the risk. Be polite, and leave on a high note.

Checklist

1. In an interview situation, you must concentrate harder than at any time in your life. To lose the thread for an instant could be disastrous.
2. Read about and practise body language. Have you ever said of someone you have recently met, 'I don't know why, I just like him'? That is your subconscious talking. Affect your interviewer's subconscious with body language.
3. Be positive. Always talk in terms of what will happen *when* you are in the post, not *if* you get the post. 'If' is a very negative word.
4. Remember to score your points on your A4 pad as you make them. It will do wonders for your enthusiasm. Do not let the interviewer see you doing this – he will think you are scoring him and will be offended.
5. At each and every interview, give it everything you have. Work for success until it hurts.

Chapter 9
The Personnel Department

Your first visit to company headquarters will be an exciting experience. It will be your first taste of the flavour of your future employer, your first sight of the building in which you will work, and your first meeting with future working colleagues. How will you know that you are meeting future colleagues? You won't, and that is the whole crux of the matter. You will be on show, and everyone or no one will be asked to make an assessment of you. That alone will be enough to keep you alert and on your toes.

The Personnel receptionist

It is likely that the first person you meet on your visit to company headquarters will be the receptionist in Personnel. She may be a staff member with simple responsibility for reception, or she may be a trained personnel officer filling in for the lunch break. You will not know, so it is important that you start off on the right foot.

Approach the desk or counter, put your bag on the floor and announce yourself in a friendly open-faced manner. Tell her why you are there, and who you have come to see. She will indicate what her instructions are, but it is likely she will ask you to sit, offer you a cup of tea or coffee, and notify the department of your arrival. Arrive early, say 10 minutes. Too early may indicate a lack of organizational skill.

It is not unusual to be asked to sign a chit for travel expenses at this time. Do not claim for expenses you have not made, or put in inflated figures. For all you know, the Personnel Officer might make the same journey twice a week. Another applicant might have made the same journey from the same town. Be warned.

Killing time in the reception area

When you have been attended to, see if you can find an in-house journal. Scan it quickly. You are looking for an ice-breaker, perhaps news of a big important order, or details of progress on the new factory site. Look for something of which the company is justifiably proud. Ask if you can keep the publication so you can let your future interviewers know later on that you have it.

This shows interest and is a good scoring point. If there isn't one, then ask. They may have run out. Nothing at all? Then take out some information on the company or product that you obtained from PR on your research programme.

Are there other people in reception? Candidates for the same position? There may well be, but don't just sit there and ignore them. Get into conversation, but reveal nothing important about yourself; if they ask what job you are applying for, then lie. They will be put off guard, and you can ask questions that they would not normally answer. I have found that telling them I am a behavioural psychologist asked to attend a series of interviews on that day has a strongly marked effect on their confidence, and gets them talking quite freely, trying to impress me, thinking they have stolen a march on the competition.

When you are called, say goodbye to your newly found friend. You may be working with him one day.

Aptitude tests – how to pass them

Many companies, especially the larger ones, put great store by aptitude tests. Plan on having to answer at least three of these and possibly four.

Always remember that there are no right answers to these. They are designed to assess your personality. They are always written tests, with a time limit for answering each one. They will contain anything up to 200 short three-choice questions. A typical question would be:

1. If a colleague didn't agree with your point of view, would you
   (a) Change your opinion?
   (b) Agree to differ?
   (c) Argue until he changed his opinion?

or:

2. If you took up a spare-time hobby, would you choose
   (a) A team sport?
   (b) An individual sport?
   (c) Avoid sport altogether?

In answering these questions, bear in mind the profile people look for. They want someone who can get along with his fellows, but is not afraid to stick to his principles: a well-disciplined man who can work in a team but apply his own personality to the task; a man who will adhere to company policy, but is not afraid to stick his neck out for the good of the company when a clear policy statement is un-available. A middle-of-the-road man? Perhaps, but that shade of individuality is all important. If they wanted a clone, you wouldn't be there. Let your answers show a tempered aggression, a dynamo waiting for the action. Show gentleness when it is appropriate, strength when needed.

Getting the results

Knowing how you did in the tests is as important as doing them. If you are not told on the day, then ring two or three days later and ask. Your enthusiasm will be noted and an encouraging result will be good for your morale.

Not all tests are of the simple type. Some are word tests that take account of your knowledge of English, some are mathematical to measure your capability to make assessments of a situation, test concentration and discover whether you think logically. Some are extremely complicated and would only be completed fully and correctly by a genius. These are designed to test your powers of switching from one task to another totally unrelated one, say from analysing a proposal to making sense of production figures.

The purpose of Personnel

The Personnel Department is often referred to as a management tool. It is their job to make the system work, where it applies to people. They design and implement the various systems in force to cater for all aspects of human management.

They are the ones, therefore, to explain the remuneration package, the pension scheme, holidays, expense reclamation, all the nuts and bolts that hold the whole deal together. Remember this when you put together your list of questions. Remember also our decisions on the money question. If they mention a salary scale, do not question it at this time, but neither should you agree it.

It is also not uncommon for there to be some difference between facts as stated by Personnel and facts on the same subject as stated by later interviewers. This arises when the specification on the package is yet to be finalized. Make a note of the anomalies and raise them at the final interview. Don't get into pointless arguments at this stage.

Finally, do not neglect to go through the final routine of restating the benefits and asking if he has any reservations as to your suitability for the post. It is as important to make up the mind of the Personnel Officer, who, incidentally, is often a woman these days, as it is to make up the mind of the UK or Departmental Manager. Neither should you forget to send another letter, along the lines of the last, stating your thanks and enthusiasm for the job. Once again, it is the little things that count.

Checklist

1. Visit your local library and learn what you can about aptitude tests. Forewarned is forearmed and any fear you may have of this subject will be dispelled when you discover that it is an inexact science that only works on broad terms.
2. Prepare a list of questions for the Personnel Department that will give you answers dealing with the nuts and bolts of the position. For example, pension details, working hours, medical health plan, and so on.
3. Be careful not to downgrade the Personnel interview. Do not forget to 'close the sale' just because you have been discussing mundane topics.

Chapter 10
The UK Manager
Interview

Most senior managers are unsuited to interview and select personnel, but it is the one area that they can never keep their noses out of. No doubt they would say they had a vested interest in the selection of their executives, but the real reason, I suspect, is the enjoyment to be had from exercising power and authority. If this point is borne in mind at interview, the fears associated with being interviewed by the top man will melt away. The main point to remember is that you must treat him with care and precision. A tiny error may upset him, and the lack of courage to argue with him displayed by his subordinates may cost you the job. For that reason, then, this one must go right.

Why now?

Not all interviews with the manager holding UK responsibility occur in the early stages of the selection procedure, but it does happen simply because his time is limited and the schedule must be built around his diary. Be aware, therefore, and do not get taken by surprise.

What is he looking for?

Frankly, he knows what he wants, because he possibly had a hand in the construction of the job specification, but he doesn't necessarily recognize it when he sees it. Your job, therefore, is to remind him of the specification and show him how well you fit it. You must then get him to agree that you fit, and send him off convinced that you are the answer to the problem. Difficult? Not at all, if you stick to the programme.

What can be gleaned from him?

A senior manager deals in overall views. Detail is not his preserve. He simply gathers information, uses that information to make a decision, then passes that decision to his management team for implementation. This he will do with you. He will be interested in the overall effect you will have on his product and the team you will be joining. Also, how you will fit a broader view of the activity of the company.

To him you must stress your suitability as an ambassador for the company, the fact that you are a 'company man' or 'company woman' as well as proving your ability to do the job.

From him you can get an overall picture of the company's future, the plans for its products, and how he sees things in the years to come. The secret is to get him talking. This is his stock in trade. It is what he does all day, every day. Most of his time is spent in presentation activity of products and management cases, so use your presentation skills competently. Stick to your planned agenda, use your visual aids, guide the interview to a decision-making conclusion, get him to agree and affirm each major point and close the sale by asking for the job.

If he says he cannot give it at this time, which is likely, then finish with the same 'suitability' question. If that brings out reservations, deal with them and ask if he is now satisfied. If he is, but still will not give you the job, then he has probably been truthful and you can do no more.

How friendly can you be?

As a top man, he will consider his position unassailable by you, and he can afford to be friendly and open. Use this situation for all it is worth. Remember the technique for gaining friendship and rapport: that is, mirroring his bodily movements, and 'bringing him along' with you. If you can get the chemistry right with this man, you will have a powerful ally should it come to a group decision, even though your qualifications and experience might not be the tops.

At this interview, you must constantly assess and reassess your impression of him and his attitude towards you. Again, total concentration is needed to catch any change of attitude in him, to be aware of any change of empathy caused by a wrong word or phrase. At this interview, as much if not more so than any other, you must appear as a congenial person who can temper business activity with humanity. Never forget, if you wish to rise up the management tree, there will always come a time when you will have to get on with people, and be able to get them to do things for you without having to lay down the law all the time. In short, you will have to get on with him. He will be looking for signs of this. Do not disappoint him.

How well did I do?

You will only know by the reluctance with which the interviewer lets you go. When he finds a good man, he starts to worry. His concern is based on the belief that you will be job-hunting elsewhere. Even if you are, and it will be counter-productive if you do (my advice is don't), never tell him in an effort to force a decision. The one thing they will not do is to allow you to blackmail them. The only way is constantly to affirm that this is the only job that you are remotely interested in, and why, and have the courage to suppress and live with your fears that all your eggs are in one basket.

Believe me, total commitment to one aim is the only way you will achieve success. Anything less will be noticed with ease, and you will end up as the second or third choice at best.

There is, however, nothing wrong in asking for a time-scale on the decision, but it is inappropriate before this interview. Knowing the time-scale will stop you worrying every time the postman passes your door.

More letters?

Of course. You would be staggered how little courtesy there is in business, and anything that puts you above the competition is worth doing. Another thank-you letter then, affirming your interest and conviction and pent-up enthusiasm to get started.

Checklist

Apart from bearing in mind all that has been suggested in previous lists, one major point needs stressing here: *image*. You are before a top man. You must display an image reconcilable with a competent, thoughtful, totally dedicated businessman or woman. This must be recognized from the way you look, the way you present your case, and your obvious commitment to his company, and, above all, your enthusiasm.

Chapter 11

The Departmental Manager Interview

This is it. This is what you have been working for. You are going to be interviewed by your new boss.

Everything that has been said before regarding appearance, punctuality, empathy, enthusiasm and commitment now counts double.

How to greet him

Make no mistake, he has heard of you. He has seen your CV. He has seen the results of your tests. He has had assessments of your worth from previous interviewers and he has seen your competition. I will stake my all that he has been awaiting this meeting with gathering excitement for days. Do not disappoint him. Greet him with the enthusiasm of a long-lost dear friend. To this man, chemistry is everything. If you have got this far, he doesn't give a damn about your experience, qualifications or anything else. He is a seat-of-the-pants flyer. He will know in five minutes if you are the man or woman for him. In most cases, in my experience, it has been less. The rest of the interview is just pure pleasure for him because he realizes that his search is over. The two minds have met. The irresistible force – you – has collided with the immovable object – him – and that collision must be seen to occur.

Do not rush to greet him, but make damn sure that he knows that it is only because wild horses are holding you back.

What to talk about

You are going to do a job for him. He wants to know how you are going to do it. Your presentation of your own personal market plan, how you see it, how you are going to implement it, how you will monitor it, must all be based on the information you have obtained from previous interviews and research. Without a doubt, that input has come, at first instance, from him. He wants you to bring it back to him with all the spaces coloured in, all the flesh put on to the bones. The only way to do this effectively is to role-play it beforehand. Practise your presentation. Practise your delivery.

The subjective influence

When an interviewer meets the answer to his problems, it is very difficult for him to remain objective. He will sing your praises to all who will listen, he will take a firm stance at the meetings that will follow, he will even put his authority to the test and state categorically that you are the person he wants. He has to work with you, so his opinion will carry massive weight. You must play on the subjective. You must establish a rapport that will make it difficult for him to envisage a complete team without your inclusion. To do this is easier than it might appear.

The hot button

That phrase will be instantly recognizable to the salesmen among us. It refers to the motivation within us all to perform an act or take a decision. This hot button is the most important point to bring out. You must search for it by asking questions until you find the most important thing in his life regarding the appointment of a new member of the team.

Looking back at our example, George will be employed to set up a distribution network. When the best way to get the product to the end-user was being considered, the Marketing Manager was strongly against using a simple direct-sales activity to move the product, favouring a distribution network because of the long-term benefits in respect of a base to sell other products still in the pipeline. His wishes were acceded to. He must make that distribution network perform. That is his hot button.

When George talks to him, he will concentrate on this, linking every action to the end result, showing how it will achieve this, constantly 'pushing the button' until the Manager gets so fired up with enthusiasm that he takes the desired action and employs George because he is convinced that that is the only way that he can get a result.

Discovering that hot button can only be done by questioning, and you should start your search as early as possible. The sooner you have found it, the longer time there is available to push it. You can never push it too much.

The team and how to contribute

No matter what the activity or job, you will be joining a team. The second most important thing to get across is that you will be a contributing, active member of a team. To do this, never speak of *you*, always *we*. Emphasize the fact that you know a competent, established team is already in place, and you are joining it to complement that team and increase its effectiveness. You are an individual with fresh ideas and a goal to reach, but you are not a lone wolf.

Making his job easier

He has, at the end of the day, to make a decision. Make it easy for him. Use the interview period to affirm with him the qualities needed for a successful filling of the post. Agree those qualities with him. Restate those qualities, matching them with your own and showing how yours will give the desired result. When you have finished, once more ask if he has any reservations about your suitability. Make the decision easy for him, and solve the objections to your appointment at the same time. He will start, as you talk, to think of you as an indispensable tool for the task. Once he does this, the battle is yours. He will have no problem in converting a subjective opinion to an objective analysis when it comes to a group decision.

Before you leave, it is most important that you tell him how much you look forward to working *for* him and *with* his team. Do not get these words the wrong way round, or presume, at this stage, that you are working *with* him. Managers are very aware of the reporting chain and resent deeply any threat to it. If he feels that, in the early stages, you have the wrong impression as to your proper place in the chain, it will undo all the good work that you have done. Later, yes, you will work together very closely, and a bond will be created, but tread warily at first.

Not another letter?

But of course, and do not fall into the trap of making all these letters read exactly the same. Each must be worded differently to have the proper effect, but the message is always the same: unalloyed pleasure at the thought of working for the one company that you would consider joining, and total commitment to making the job a success.

Checklist

1. For this interview, you must role-play it.
2. Practise getting your plans over.
3. Practise your presentation and delivery.
4. Work hard on visual aids and their use if you employ them.
5. Search, search, search for that hot button, and keep pushing it.
6. Accentuate your knowledge that you will be part of a team, and your eagerness to make that situation work.
7. Avoid the impression that you will work *with* him. Now is not the time to threaten his position, no matter how ambitious you are.

Chapter 12

They Come in Pairs – the Final Meeting

Sooner or later, the final interview will arrive. It could be at the end of a gruelling series of six interviews or perhaps after just one, but whatever the time-scale, there will be no avoiding it. The one advantage is that all the questions will already have been asked. Ninety-nine per cent of all final interviews consist of a restatement of subject matter that has gone before. Because of this, you are on a winner. Had your answers been wrong the first time, you would not be invited back. Capitalize on this by feeling totally confident, free of all nervousness, and exude unbounded enthusiasm.

If it has not been indicated that this will be the final interview (and it usually is) you will know the moment you enter the room. Two people will be sitting there, and you will already have met them. It is more than likely that they will be the Personnel Manager and the Departmental Manager, your new boss.

Remember all that has gone before. Do not change anything. Stick to your plans for the job. However, come prepared to explain it all over again, as if you had never met.

Do not worry about being faced with two people, or even more. Always answer direct to the person who asked the question. Bear in mind that only one man can speak at once. Listen to the question, *think before you answer*, then speak slowly and decisively. By speaking slowly, you will stop the session turning into a rapid-fire exchange, which will only fluster you and force you into a mistake.

A clue to your progress can always be obtained by the length of any interview. If you are still there after half an hour, you are only achieving the average, but at least you haven't been dismissed out of hand. Three-quarters of an hour is encouraging. Lasting the full hour is splendid. That is how long most interviews are planned. If it overruns, and it is not doing so because you are dragging it out, then you are winning, and winning hands down. They are finding you so interesting that they are prepared to make the next candidate, if there is one, wait until they are ready.

At some point in the final interview where two people are acting together, they will ask you to leave the room. Then you will know that a decision is about to be made. It is very often the case that if you are to be appointed, you will be told at interview. Very rarely are you sent home to await notification by letter. The whole case is too risky for the employer. He could very well lose you, and he is not prepared to do that and take the chance of never finding a better replacement: perhaps a touch of the bird in the hand being better than two in the bush. Remember, he started out with a bulging aviary.

While you are away, one of two things is happening. They are either congratulating themselves on their good fortune, or one of the interviewers is not quite convinced. Unless everything has gone wrong, it is highly unlikely that both are having second thoughts. You must be prepared for a wait of anything up to 20 minutes.

When you are asked to return, you must be as alert as a tiger stalking its prey. You may well be asked to clarify a point or two, but this is window dressing. Be assured, the decision has been made. When it comes, in your favour, restrain yourself from jumping around the room, but smile gently and happily, get up, and extend your hand, thanking your new boss first if he is present. He will never forget your allegiance to him and no better start can be made.

If you have managed successfully to avoid the question of salary until this point, now is the time to deal with it.

Fight hard, do not be afraid to state your case. Your respect within the company will never be higher than it is now for some time to come. At last, you hold the reins.

The job offer

Either at the end of this interview, or a few days later, you will be given a formal letter offering you the job and stating the terms. You may be asked to sign a copy and return it. Do not leave this action to be your way of thanking them for employing you.

Write again, when you return home, thanking them for employing you, affirming your intention to do well and perform all the tasks in the manner that you have intimated, and looking forward to a long and happy career with the company, and address it to your new boss. Leave him with the feeling that he has employed the right man for the job, and that you will never let him down.

Checklist

1. Never fear the two-person interview. It is a sign that the long haul is nearly over, and up to this point you have been successful. It is a time to rejoice. Think of all the others who did not make it.
2. Avoid the rapid-fire exchanges by thinking before you answer questions and taking your time.
3. If you are asked questions that have occurred before, give the same answers, but make sure that you have rephrased them. Avoid repetition and giving the impression that you have conducted yourself parrot-fashion from a prepared script.

Chapter 13
A New Beginning

Once the offer has been made, and you are appointed, things will start to move with speed.

It is not unusual for a selection programme to take three months, but once the company have chosen, they always want you on board yesterday. Don't delay. Take up your position as soon as you possibly can.

Most jobs start with a product training programme and induction schedule. Be prepared to spend time away from home in an hotel for anything from three days to four weeks, depending on the job and your product knowledge and experience. All expenses will be paid. Do not be afraid to ask the accounts division, or your boss, for an expense float to cover this period.

On your first day, you will be asked to produce any formal qualifications if the post is technical, birth and marriage certificates for the pension fund application, driving licence for your company car, bank account number and sort code for your salary and your P.45 from your last employer for your tax details.

If the production of a P.45 is going to cause you problems because of unemployment that you felt it important to skip over, then use this system.

Before applying for the job, ring your local tax office and tell them that you are going to start a company and will employ staff on a PAYE basis, so you need all the relevant forms and tax tables. In the package they will send you will be a number of P.45 forms and instructions on how to fill them in. A file code number will also be given you for use on all documentation. Never register your business under your own name. Do not concern yourself with limited companies.

When you sign off as unemployed, the P.45 you will be given is clearly identifiable as coming from the unemployment benefit office of the Department of Employment. Simply copy the details from the old P.45 on to the new one, taking instructions from the *blue card* that will be included in your tax package, putting the date of leaving your own new company as the date you are starting with the new employer. Wait a further week, then hand the new P.45 to your payroll clerk.

This system is not illegal, but should only be used if you have no other option. Those whom it affects will know what I mean.

Once you join your company, remember that you are the new man, and act accordingly. Take time for people to get to know you. Make a conscious effort to fit into the team. Sit quietly and absorb everything around you, noting who reports to whom, and when, and for what.

Do not be afraid to ask questions, however simple they may seem to you. Do not be controversial, and keep your opinions to yourself unless asked for them. When asked, be non-committal on general subjects. Mistakes made at this time can be irreparable and mar your acceptance for a long time to come.

Lastly, deliver the goods. Work like a Trojan for the first four months. Make yourself indispensable. Help everyone you can, and you can look forward to a long and happy career.

Words of commiseration?

There are none in this book. I believe there is no place for them. If you didn't get the job, simply start over again, looking for a new opportunity, beginning the whole process once more. If you work hard enough, you have an excellent chance of being successful first time, but no system is 100 per cent foolproof.

Accept the fact that if you failed in your endeavour, then it was your fault. Something you did or did not do, something you said or did not say, was wrong.

Go over it in your mind. Every step of the way. Be honest with yourself, and you will find the answer.

A positive mental attitude

This is what it comes down to. The man or woman with PMA stands out like a lighthouse on a foggy night, and shines as brightly to his or her fellows. It instils a power within that has the force to move mountains. PMA is contagious. It affects all who come in contact with you. It lifts their hearts and minds to your plane. They see things with your eyes and are the more excited for it. They want to be a part of your scene, they feel the vibrations. Not everyone will understand what you mean when you tell them that it is all down to PMA. They are used to calling it by its common name...

ENTHUSIASM